"I am so grateful for a daily devotional that honors both scripture and real life. Jha offers us a real jewel here, a way to root ourselves in The Word while not having to put on some kind of petty piety to do it. This devotional is magically pastoral and realistic. I really can't wait to use it!" —**Nadia Bolz-Weber,** *New York Times* **bestselling author**

"Sandhya Jha has given us a devotional that is at once both comforting and challenging. In these times, we need more than ever to be reminded not only of the unconditional love of Jesus, but of his commandment to love boldly and courageously to bring liberation to all the world." —**Terri Hord Owens, General Minister and President, Christian Church (Disciples of Christ)**

"*Liberating Love* by Sandhya Rani Jha is the devotional that so many of us have been waiting to arrive. Through the carefully chosen scripture passages and thoughtful messages of solidarity and kindness in God's voice, I felt seen, known, and cared for by a God that can often feel far awa' ⌐here is no sorting through condemning, exclusionary theolr 'uring shallow reflections, only the gift of words that ? 'vine sees and values my life and accompanies ₃—a gift we can all use as we meet a world r ₎pression." —**Micky ScottBey Jones, the Justic'**

"I love this book. I have plenty r collected during the years. My all-time favori' .y nightstand. This book will surely find a space. .g style is refreshing, inviting, and leaves a lasting in, .₁ one's heart. I highly recommend this book for your nights. —**Sharon Risher, author of** *For Such a Time as This*

"*Liberating Love: A Daily Devotional* is a theological telescope for the soul. Rev. Jha dynamically extends and rearranges lenses to illuminate the kind of light that connects the beloved community with the deeply rooted gifts of scripture. The arc of justice-making and community-building is long. She brilliantly feeds us sustenance for each day as she carefully reminds us of the ways that we are liberated by and for community." —**Yvonne T. Gilmore, Disciples Divinity House of the University of Chicago, Reconciliation Ministry**

"In a world that too often feels like it is plunging into chaos, Sandhya Jha's steady voice calls us back to intimacy with a God who is both capable of shaping a world from the formless void and of holding our broken hearts in tender hands. This lovely book reminds us that God is always seeking to summon us into the joy of a new creation where peace and justice bind us together in a community that finds its home in God's expansive love." —**Derek Penwell, author of** *Outlandish: An Unlikely Messiah, a Messy Ministry, and the Call to Mobilize*

"In a time when we need more than ever to remember we belong to one another, these beautiful, authentic devotions bring God's hope for community straight to our hearts. Written with refreshing personal conviction and disarming tenderness, this devotional will set you free and empower you toward a life of love over fear. Sandhya Rani Jha ignites in us both the possibilities and divine presence embedded within as she makes God's voice accessible and empowering. She pushes us to see all of Scripture as a collective call toward the heartbeat of God, one that steadily beats for those who are forgotten." —**Arianne Braithwaite Lehn, author of** *Ash and Starlight: Prayers for the Chaos and Grace of Daily Life*

"It is time to be still and read *Liberating Love: 365 Love Notes From God*. You will find new life in God's love notes written just for you: words of compassion, encouragement, hope, and love. In these poetic, prophetic, and faithful devotions of love you will experience spiritual liberation. The world needs these love notes from God now more than ever." —**Sarah Griffith Lund, author of** *Blessed Are the Crazy: Breaking the Silence about Mental Illness, Family, and Church*

SANDHYA RANI JHA

Liberating Love

365 LOVE NOTES FROM GOD

A Daily Devotional

chalice
press

Saint Louis, Missouri

An imprint of Christian Board of Publication

Dearest Aeryn,
I LOVE YOU!!! Thank
you for being a part of
my ordination service. I
am blessed to call you
my sister in Christ.
♡ Rev. Riana

Cover design: Jennifer Pavlovitz
Interior design: Connie H.C. Wang
Photo on back cover: Cindy Manly-Fields

ChalicePress.com

Print: 9780827221963
EPUB: 9780827221970
EPDF: 9780827221987

Printed in the United States of America

Contents

Preface vi

January 1

February 32

March 61

April 92

May 122

June 153

July 183

August 214

September 245

October 275

November 306

December 336

Conclusion 367

Index 370

Preface

A friend of mine gave me a very popular daily devotional a few years ago to support my commitment to a deeper relationship with Christ. It was very sweet and very personal. The intent of the writer moved me deeply because the writer wanted every person to have a deep individual relationship with Jesus that led them to be a better individual. It was like most devotionals in this way—seemingly apolitical, oriented toward "me and Jesus," and a little dose of encouragement for a person of faith dealing with the hardships of being human...and not really oriented toward the creating of God's kindom[1] here on earth, which is a message that shows up in almost every passage in the Bible but in very little devotional literature.

As I was picking the devotional up to take to the free book table at the nonprofit I run, I found myself thinking, "I wish there were a devotional like this for the rest of us...a devotional that connects us not just individually to Jesus but to each other, reminding us that every one of us was made in the image of God. A devotional that respects the scripture enough not to engage it literally, but to actually take it seriously."

And although I was alone in my apartment, I distinctly heard a voice say, "Yes. You need to do that."

I received that word just before my father was rushed to the hospital and then ended up dying without ever regaining consciousness. I wrote about a quarter of it at Johns Hopkins Hospital in Baltimore. It was a gift

---

[1] I use the word *kindom* because most of us cannot relate to a world with a king and because we know God is not one particular gender, as a king usually is, but we can possibly relate to a world where we are each other's siblings or kin, which is a vision of heaven Jesus cast for us regularly. It is a personal preference I learned from womanist theologians maybe 15 years ago.

to stay grounded in the scripture[2] so that I was accompanied during that time and the time after by ancestors who knew hope and promise and grief and loneliness and companionship and hard times and comfort. It was also a gift to write it while surrounded by healers: the doctors and nurses, the cleaning and administrative staff, the chaplain, the woman who signed in visitors to the critical care unit. All were instrumental parts of the whole care process they sought to bring to patients, many of whom would not make it. They all influenced how aware I was of God as Healer while writing this devotional.

I want to acknowledge Pastor Larry Love from the farming community of Woodland, California, who is so committed to church folks understanding that God has ALWAYS sought our best lives and thriving, not JUST in the New Testament, and that God is almost chasing us to make sure we know God's love. Larry wrote a curriculum called *Dash Through the Bible* that people from my denomination studied across northern California in 2007. His subtle ways of teaching us to reject the anti-Semitic message that the Bible is about a vengeful Hebrew God of laws and a gentle New Testament God of love helped me reengage the Bible in such a life-giving way. Additionally, the illustrated book *Mannah in the Wilderness* was introduced to me by Rev. Deb Conrad from Flint, Michigan, when we were working with young adults volunteering with our denomination during the summer of 2016. I loved it so much that I assigned it to my niece as homework when she got in trouble and had to volunteer at my nonprofit the next winter. Finally, part of the theme of this devotional is about how the Bible speaks to us as community over and over. When I needed to do a final edit of this devotional, I couldn't imagine catching all the glitches by reading 366 devotions in a row myself, so I reached out to 11 friends so we could each take one month. My profound thanks to Riana Shaw Robinson, Kristi Laughlin, Yvonne Gilmore, Alan Dicken, Larry Morris, Chesla Nickelson, Jim Mitulski, Tuhina Rasche, Cinthia Kim Hengst, Amy Fourrier, and Gabriel Lopez. It takes a village to understand God's word, and it took a village to create a devotional.

---

[2](I used the *New Revised Standard Version,* NRSV, because it's the closest translation to the original, although in my own worship I often use the inclusive translation, and I also really love the *Jewish Study Bible.*)

And after all, it took years of wrestling with the text in community for me to begin to attempt something like this. As Riana said to me, "this devotion is a gift for community, from community." At its best, that is how we connect with the divine as well: in and through and with one another.

* * *

I went to a church where we read portions of every book of the Bible when I was in fourth grade and again when I was in eighth. I read the vast majority again when I was in seminary, with lots of additional information to better understand the times in which it was written. And yet the great gift of God placing this task on my shoulders was reconnecting with the old friends of these books, the ones I don't hang out with as much these days: Jonah and Demetrius and King Cyrus and Hannah. As I researched passages and began writing devotions, I couldn't wait for others to get to hang out with those same friends.

My challenge in writing this faithfully was that so much is taken out of context in most devotionals; things meant for communities are warped to be only about individuals, when most of scripture is a guidebook on how to be God's people PLURAL, not just God's person SINGULAR. I want to connect people to the vibrant and living stories in the text, and it can be hard to inspire and not reduce the experience to lectures about historical context. This is why so many devotionals either end up being nonsubstantive, literal, or pedantic.

I tried my best to honor the life-giving stories of the Bible that still inspire me. I tried not to pull things out of context. I also skipped some really complicated texts that require a lot of interpretation because this isn't the place for debate. God put on my heart the task of encouragement and hope and loving support in ways that do not place any of these texts above others, even though I have my own interpretations borne of deep study and deep prayer.

One of the things I was confronted with when reading the whole Bible (and you might be also, if you do): there were camps, teams, sides in the debate, because the Bible was written across time, as people were nuancing what it meant to be in community. Sometimes one rule would be REALLY important to preserving God's community, and other times almost its opposite was absolutely critical to protect the community. As we read the text, though, we don't think about how circumstances have changed and community needs have changed, and how different ideologies had the scrolls and ink. Here are a few examples of those competing beliefs that showed up as I read the Bible as one whole document, and how those different beliefs could show up almost as if the Bible were arguing with itself from chapter to chapter:

- Keep separate from non-Jews so the faith isn't corrupted.
- Don't shut out the foreigner.
- Sodom and Gomorrah were about sexual depravity.
- Sodom and Gomorrah were about a city that was without compassion.
- Follow the rules.
- Follow love.
- Follow the rules because of love.
- People who have been forced into slavery should be treated well.
- People who have been forced into slavery should be free.
- People who have been forced into slavery should tolerate whatever treatment they are given.
- God is furious and will destroy you.
- God is all compassion and mercy.

And note: these are not "angry God in the Hebrew Bible" and "merciful God in the New Testament." These tensions exist throughout the whole Bible as God's people were figuring out how to be God's people, and since I chose to use scriptures from the entire Bible, those tensions were a real challenge as I thought through God's relationship to each scripture.

The thing that shows up indisputably, though, is the thousands of references to helping the poor and the widow and the orphan and the foreigner, and the call to treating workers well. The reason I am thankful God placed this task on my shoulders is this: I got the unexpected and long overdue luxury of living in the texts for a long stretch of time. There is a reason God's storybook endures. It is not magic. It is not only (I hope this doesn't sound heretical) that it is God's will that it endure. These stories from long ago are true to our time as well—a time of complexity and wrestling and longing and hope and struggling and overcoming, a time of God showing up in the midst of everything we face.

I hope it is not too presumptuous, but I did choose to write this devotional as if each devotion were written to you, the reader, by God. When you read the word "I" in the devotion, the "I" is my imagining of how God might talk about the scripture and God's relationship to you. I hope God doesn't think this is too presumptuous, and I hope it helps you engage your own relationship with God in some life-giving ways.

It is my earnest prayer that you find, within these pages, encouragement and inspiration, and that you feel connected to our all-loving God, to our spiritual ancestors, and also to your siblings, God's children all over the world. That, I believe, was the task God gave me, and if I succeeded in even the smallest way, I am grateful to have been given the chance.

January

January 1

Genesis 1:1-3

• • •

In the beginning when God created the heavens and the earth, the earth was a formless void and darkness covered the face of the deep, while a wind from God swept over the face of the waters. Then God said, "Let there be light"; and there was light.

• • •

I was there from the beginning, and I was there from *your* beginning. Today is a day for us to restart our journey together, and this I promise: I will always provide light for the journey. Today, I invite you to take a moment and revel in my creation, and to find ways to honor it and care for it. This is what I seek for us together this year: that you might grow closer to me and creation and that you might always feel my light around and inside you, even in the hard seasons. *If I could create all of this, what can't I create in you?*

January 2

Matthew 2:13–15

• • •

Now after they had left, an angel of the Lord appeared to Joseph in a dream and said, "Get up, take the child and his mother, and flee to Egypt, and remain there until I tell you; for Herod is about to search for the child, to destroy him." Then Joseph got up, took the child and his mother by night, and went to Egypt, and remained there until the death of Herod. This was to fulfill what had been spoken by the Lord through the prophet, "Out of Egypt I have called my son."

• • •

From the first days of my Son's life, there were risks and threats and people who feared him. This world fears the power of Love. Today, I invite you to ask how you can be like Egypt, opening yourself to the forces of Love knocking at your door, fleeing to you. I created you as generous and compassionate. And I know this world will try to place fear in your heart. In order to walk closely with me, I ask you to find ways to embrace my Love and reject the forces of fear. Because, my beloved child, I made you for Love. You deserve Love.

January 3

Exodus 1:15–17

• • •

The king of Egypt said to the Hebrew midwives, one of whom was named Shiphrah and the other Puah, "When you act as midwives to the Hebrew women, and see them on the birthstool, if it is a boy, kill him; but if it is a girl, she shall live." But the midwives feared God; they did not do as the king of Egypt commanded them, but they let the boys live.

• • •

You have sisters, too many to name, who have served me for generations by protecting my most vulnerable children. Some of them have even been a little sneaky in order to protect the weak from those who would do them harm. You have survived vulnerable times, and I am so glad that you are here, now, a survivor, ready to be a midwife to my vulnerable children today. I invite you to pay attention to my other midwives (of all genders) around you today, so you know you are never alone in this calling.

January 4

Mark 1:16–18

• • •

As Jesus passed along the Sea of Galilee, he saw Simon and his brother Andrew casting a net into the sea—for they were fishermen. And Jesus said to them, "Follow me and I will make you fish for people." And immediately they left their nets and followed him.

• • •

All you have done in your life to this point, all of your experiences, the joyful ones and the painful ones, have equipped you for this moment. I have called you, and here you are seeking to follow. Fishers and tax collectors and sex workers and homemakers and kings and people forced into slavery have all done my will across the generations, and you are an inheritor of their legacy. I invite you today to pay attention to how what you are doing now may be of service to my will in this aching, hurting world.

January 5

Leviticus 19:32

• • •

You shall rise before the aged, and defer to the old; and you shall fear your God: I am the LORD.

• • •

I take so much joy in all of my children, from newborn infants to the oldest of elders. This world sometimes forgets that there are gifts in every generation. Sometimes this world only values the fast and the productive. This world has forgotten what I want you to reflect on today: I do not value you for your productivity. I value you for your faithfulness, your humility, your vulnerability, your compassion, your service. I invite you to look around today and notice the people I love whom this world has forgotten to treasure. And I invite you first to look in the mirror.

January 6

Luke 2:48-49

• • •

When [Jesus'] parents saw him they were astonished; and his mother said to him, "Child, why have you treated us like this? Look, your father and I have been searching for you in great anxiety." He said to them, "Why were you searching for me? Did you not know that I must be in my Father's house?"

• • •

Seek me where my Son sought me: in the rich debates and dialogues and disagreements that faithful people can have when they are seeking to understand me. At the age of 12, my Son engaged wise rabbis, debating the fine points of how to honor me best. Do not hide from the discussion as if any one of my children can understand me by themselves. Distrust my children who have been led astray and believe they have the answers. I created you for each other. Only in wrestling with my word *together* can you grow closer to my heart's wish for you. I will tell you a secret, and I invite you to ponder it today: my wisdom does not lie within any one of you. My word rests *between* you.

January 7

Numbers 5:5–7

• • •

The Lord spoke to Moses, saying: Speak to the Israelites: When a man or a woman wrongs another, breaking faith with the Lord, that person incurs guilt and shall confess the sin that has been committed. The person shall make full restitution for the wrong, adding one-fifth to it, and giving it to the one who was wronged.

• • •

I understand that you will sometimes drift, that you will sometimes fail those you love. I love you and I forgive you. And because you are my child, I know you are capable of acknowledging your failings and of seeking to make them right. I am not a God of retribution; from the beginnings of creation I have been a God of restoration, including the restoration of relationships. Today I invite you to reflect on where you have drifted, where you have failed someone, and how you can find out how to make it right, for the sake of following me.

January 8

John 1:5

• • •

The light shines in the darkness, and the darkness did not overcome it.

• • •

These days are short; there is a lot of darkness. And I know that these can be some of the hardest days to face. I want to remind you that because of people like you, my light has never disappeared in the hardest of days. It has always been there to light the path for people facing their own shadows or the shadows of fear, pain, and heartbreak. Today I invite you to reflect on how my beloved Son came to shine a light that still shines today. And I invite you to reflect on how that light shines in you for those who need it, and where you can invite me in to shine more brightly in your own life. Because I want to be there now; I have always wanted to be there.

January 9

Deuteronomy 1:17a

• • •

You must not be partial in judging: hear out the small and the great alike; you shall not be intimidated by anyone, for the judgment is God's.

• • •

I know there have been times you have felt misunderstood. No one can know anyone's entire story except for me. That is why, throughout the scriptures, I kept reminding your ancestors, your forebears, that they do not get to judge people whose stories they do not yet know. And now I remind you. Prejudging is absolutely a sin; judging with limited information is a sin. And favoring those in power over those who are struggling is not only a sin; it breaks my heart. Today I invite you to think of my children who are being prejudged, judged without people having full knowledge of their situation, and ask yourself how you can play a role in compassionately liberating people from the sin of prejudgment.

January 10

Acts 2:44-45

• • •

All who believed were together and had all things in common; they would sell their possessions and goods and distribute the proceeds to all, as any had need.

• • •

That very first church dedicated to my beloved Son Jesus...how they strived to follow his teachings! And how it inspired everyone around them. Because they were a community that shared everything so that no one was in need, they exhibited a faithfulness almost unparalleled in humanity's brief history on your planet. Beloved child, I made you for community. I made you for a community where you know each other's names and show up to celebrate with each other and care for each other in times of trouble. I made you for a community so filled with love that your love pours out the doors and into the streets for the sake of my beloved children who are treated badly by this world. Today I invite you to reflect on whether you are really in such a community, and how you can make your community more like what I dream of for you.

January 11

Joshua 1:5

• • •

No one shall be able to stand against you all the days of your life. As I was with Moses, so I will be with you; I will not fail you or forsake you.

• • •

You might know that Moses told me he couldn't stand up to Pharaoh. I gave him the words and I gave him a brother so he would not be alone. Sometimes even when I am with you, you feel alone in scary times. I know that. And these are scary times. I am calling on you to stand up against hatred and violence and suffering. I am calling on you to name oppression to the people in the highest levels of government who participate in or endorse those acts, like I did with Moses. I understand it feels like too much. And so I invite you today to reflect on the hard times in your own life when someone has shown up for you, or when you could feel my presence. Know that you can trust that to happen, and that I will always be with you in the times you stand for what is right.

January 12

Romans 2:2-4

• • •

You say, "We know that God's judgment on those who do such things is in accordance with truth." Do you imagine, whoever you are, that when you judge those who do such things and yet do them yourself, you will escape the judgment of God? Or do you despise the riches of his kindness and forbearance and patience? Do you not realize that God's kindness is meant to lead you to repentance?

• • •

This is the first time you're getting to meet my faithful son Paul, a Jewish convert to Christianity within a few years of my Son's murder by the government of Rome. The early churches were his whole heart, and when they broke his heart (and they did), he did not mince words. What I love about Paul, among many things, is how desperately he wanted the church to understand that my compassion toward you is not something for you to be ashamed of. My kindness is intended to lead you toward a more loving way of being in the world. The judgment, the bitterness, the lack of kindness in your generation breaks Paul's heart—and mine—to this day. Today I invite you to reflect on where you are leading with judgment instead of kindness. It may be to protect yourself, or it may be born of pride. Either way, seek my help in growing ever more into the kindness that I want you to receive, and therefore that I need you to give.

January 13

Judges 5:23 (Song of Deborah)

• • •

"Curse Meroz, says the angel of the LORD,
　　curse bitterly its inhabitants,
because they did not come to the help of the LORD,
　　to the help of the LORD against the mighty."

• • •

There came a day when my people would no longer simply turn to me in times of struggle; they demanded judges, not knowing that I remain the ultimate judge. One of the most faithful judges in those days was my treasured daughter Deborah. And in this song of prayer during a time her people (my people) had turned from me, she called many people to account for not standing with me. But here's what I want you to remember today: part of their sin was trusting in the power of humanity instead of my power. Their sin was siding with the big guy instead of knowing that I show up over and over for and with the vulnerable and never with the oppressors who harm the weak. Today I invite you to reflect on the places you are vulnerable: ask me in, ask for help. And reflect on the places you have been afraid to side with others who are vulnerable because you seek the protection of the strong. Ask me for strength to stand with the vulnerable.

January 14

1 Corinthians 2:1–3

• • •

When I came to you, brothers and sisters, I did not come proclaiming the mystery of God to you in lofty words or wisdom. For I decided to know nothing among you except Jesus Christ, and him crucified. And I came to you in weakness and in fear and in much trembling.

• • •

My message of love and vulnerability was a hard one for my son Paul to sell to a community shaped by the cloud of the Roman Empire, where what mattered was brute force, power, and a reign of fear. Paul took a lot of risks by bringing a message that transparently said my Son was murdered by the government as if he were a political prisoner, and that what seemed like a defeat for me was actually a victory. These days, your generation wears cross necklaces as a proud declaration of your devotion to Jesus, but in the early days the cross was a mark of shame. And my son Paul showed up in community saying, "I am not strong, and I follow a God who was murdered by the state." My beloved child, do you know what? That message meant something to many people who could relate to feeling vulnerable themselves, to learning that their God did not see their vulnerability as a flaw but as a thing that could help them extend the love and empathy that I dream of for you and your whole human family. Today I invite you to reflect on how your vulnerability can bring comfort to others, knowing that I love your own vulnerability.

January 15

Ruth 1:16–17

• • •

But Ruth said,
"Do not press me to leave you
    or to turn back from following you!
Where you go, I will go;
    where you lodge, I will lodge;
your people shall be my people, / and your God my God.
Where you die, I will die— / there will I be buried.
May the Lord do thus and so to me, / and more as well,
if even death parts me from you!"

• • •

I love how to this very day this passage about my faithful servant Ruth is used in wedding ceremonies all over the world as people commit themselves fully to each other. What people sometimes forget is that part of the reason this beautiful story ended up in the Bible is because my children had forgotten my teaching to love the stranger and show compassion for the foreigner. This story of Ruth's deep commitment to her mother-in-law (who came from a different culture) was intended to remind them (and you) that people different from you can model for you the deepest commitment, love, and faith, and can give you strength in hard times. I meant you to know all the beautiful diversity of my creation. I made you in my image, and I am so big that I needed billions of people to capture the fullness of my divinity. I invite you today to reflect on how you can deepen your connections to the people, the parts of my image you don't yet know.

January 16

2 Corinthians 2:15

• • •

For we are the aroma of Christ to God among those who are being saved and among those who are perishing.

• • •

Smells can be obnoxious and overpowering, but aromas are gentle and comforting and pleasant. My dream for the community gathered in Christ's name has been so badly damaged so many times by people who do not understand the power of gentle compassion. But my beloved son Paul reminds you today that if you have chosen to follow my Son Jesus Christ, that you have a responsibility to be that aroma. My daughter Mother Teresa knew not everyone in the street could be saved, but that those who were dying deserved to die with love and compassion surrounding them. Today I invite you to ask how you are serving as an aroma to those around you who need to be saved from something or who need compassion and love in their time of perishing.

January 17

1 Samuel 1:12–16

• • •

As she continued praying before the LORD, Eli observed her mouth. Hannah was praying silently; only her lips moved, but her voice was not heard; therefore Eli thought she was drunk. So Eli said to her, "How long will you make a drunken spectacle of yourself? Put away your wine." But Hannah answered, "No, my lord, I am a woman deeply troubled; I have drunk neither wine nor strong drink, but I have been pouring out my soul before the LORD. Do not regard your servant as a worthless woman, for I have been speaking out of my great anxiety and vexation all this time."

• • •

How strange that a man of God would mistake a faithful and desperate woman's prayers for drunkenness. How often people, and particularly women, are dismissed too quickly by those with power. How brave was Hannah to speak up for herself and demand basic dignity in the midst of her heartbreak. It is a blessing that this story remained in the Bible as a testimony to how power held by religious people can become sloppy, and how the regular faithful sometimes need to stand up and demand the dignity they deserve. Today I invite you to reflect on where you need to recognize others' desperation and not dismiss it, and where you may need for your desperation to be heard and regarded by others, that they may better support you.

January 18

Galatians 1:3–5

• • •

Grace to you and peace from God our Father and the Lord Jesus Christ, who gave himself for our sins to set us free from the present evil age, according to the will of our God and Father, to whom be the glory for ever and ever. Amen.

• • •

Freedom can take so many forms. Every generation has engaged in cruel mistreatment of my children, from the enslavement of the Israelites to the enslavement of my beloved children taken from their homes in Africa to the United States, to children harvesting cacao for candy bars today or forced to fight in wars they did not start and which many of them will not survive. My deepest desire is freedom from this manmade suffering. And there is also freedom from fear, freedom from sin, and freedom from our role in the systems that cause so much harm. Today I invite you to reflect on freedom for yourself and for others, and how those may be connected. Pray for those who still know literal enslavement and those who suffer from enslavement of the heart and mind, that you might know liberation and may guide others to liberation both physical and spiritual. Know that I will be with you to strengthen you for this task.

January 19

2 Samuel 5:1-2

• • •

Then all the tribes of Israel came to David at Hebron, and said, "Look, we are your bone and flesh. For some time, while Saul was king over us, it was you who led out Israel and brought it in. The Lord said to you: It is you who shall be shepherd of my people Israel, you who shall be ruler over Israel."

• • •

It may have been spiritual weakness that led my beloved children of Israel to seek a king so they could be like other nations instead of embracing the fact that I sought for them to be a completely different nation. And yet, I gave them a shepherd for their second king on purpose. First, you cannot be a shepherd without a certain willingness to extend kindness to sometimes stubborn and frustrating animals. Second, a shepherd is familiar with hard work that breeds a certain humility. Finally, a shepherd is a metaphor for the completely different version of leadership I sought then and continue to seek: loving and humble and not driven by ego or exceptionalism. That is the leadership I seek from you. Because by choosing to follow Christ, you have declared two things: to follow as a faithful servant, and to be part of the priesthood of all believers. Today I ask you to reflect on how your servant leadership can look like a shepherd's: both humble and strong, both compassionate and guiding toward a path of safety for those entrusted to your care.

January 20

Ephesians 2:4-7

• • •

But God, who is rich in mercy, out of the great love with which he loved us even when we were dead through our trespasses, made us alive together with Christ—by grace you have been saved— and raised us up with him and seated us with him in the heavenly places in Christ Jesus, so that in the ages to come he might show the immeasurable riches of his grace in kindness toward us in Christ Jesus.

• • •

Some of my followers like to focus on how people don't deserve my grace, but here's something I want you to remember all the time: I love you. I know you fall short. I know there are things you wish you could erase from your past and you don't think they can be erased. And the reality is that human beings are not all that great at grace, so there will be times I see your heart and know you seek to lead a new life in me and I will forgive you...but human beings who have been hurt will not be able to. Today I invite you to pray my healing power on the hearts of anyone you have hurt. I invite you to pray for my grace for any harm you have done. And I invite you to experiment with practicing the type of divine grace I know is deep within you for those who have hurt you. I do not need you to let them hurt you again. I just ask you to see if you can find a sliver of liberation for yourself as you release them from whatever you hold against them.

January 21

1 Kings 2:1–3

• • •

When David's time to die drew near, he charged his son Solomon, saying: "I am about to go the way of all the earth. Be strong, be courageous, and keep the charge of the LORD your God, walking in his ways and keeping his statutes, his commandments, his ordinances, and his testimonies, as it is written in the law of Moses, so that you may prosper in all that you do and wherever you turn."

• • •

In the books of Chronicles "walking in [my] ways" is shortened to "following [my] ordinances." I don't want you to think that my ordinances are arbitrary, though. Times have changed so that many of them do not make sense in your generation, but the only reason for my laws was to help your ancestors be a community that could care for each other and remain grounded in the path I set for them. When they walked in my ways, they flourished. When you walk in my ways and follow my ordinances, so will you. Breaking the rules is a popular sign of strength in your generation, but rules are needed to create a healthy and thriving community. So today I invite you to reflect on which rules help you walk in my ways and to which you want to recommit yourself. I also want you to consider which rules help create a community committed to my will, not just that of your reigning government, which always falls short of my glory.

January 22

Philippians 1:27–28a

• • •

Only, live your life in a manner worthy of the gospel of Christ, so that, whether I come and see you or am absent and hear about you, I will know that you are standing firm in one spirit, striving side by side with one mind for the faith of the gospel, and are in no way intimidated by your opponents.

• • •

My son Paul took many risks to share my love and the love of my beloved Son Jesus Christ throughout the Roman Empire, constantly risking his life because he felt the love of Christ so deeply. The knowledge of Jesus Christ literally saved him from a life of violence justified by his religious commitments. So often my name has been used for the sake of violence. Paul's message to the church in Philippi is my message to you and your spiritual community: I want to hear reports that you are standing together for the gospel of love, not bowing to any opponents who promote a false gospel of hate and judgment and violence. How is your faith community living into that practice together? How can you go deeper together?

January 23

2 Kings 1:2–3

• • •

Ahaziah had fallen through the lattice in his upper chamber in Samaria, and lay injured; so he sent messengers, telling them, "Go, inquire of Baal-zebub, the god of Ekron, whether I shall recover from this injury." But the angel of the LORD said to Elijah the Tishbite, "Get up, go to meet the messengers of the king of Samaria, and say to them, 'Is it because there is no God in Israel that you are going to inquire of Baal-zebub, the god of Ekron?'"

• • •

The thing that made the people of Israel distinct from all others was that they had come to learn that I am the one true God. And yet everyone around them worshiped false idols, and they were constantly getting pulled away from their relationship with me, even kings like Ahaziah. My prophets, like Elijah, constantly had to remind my people to put me before all other gods. Today I am not as worried about you or those in your community worshiping the god of Ekron. I am worried about you worshiping the god of materialism, of others' approval, of self-indulgence at the expense of the community's well-being, of personal comforts at the expense of this planet. What are the idols, the things you treasure, that come between you and me? How can we work together to banish those idols?

January 24

Colossians 1:11–12

• • •

May you be made strong with all the strength that comes from his glorious power, and may you be prepared to endure everything with patience, while joyfully giving thanks to the Father, who has enabled you to share in the inheritance of the saints in the light.

• • •

Following me—really following me—has always been a hard path. Placing community above self, placing me above popular opinion, advocating for the poor and the widow and the orphan and everyone treated badly by society, choosing to do those things in my name will mean you will have to endure being ignored or ridiculed or demonized. But it will help you find the other people who are true to my calling, and for that you will have much reason to give thanks. Finding my true followers keeps getting harder and harder when so many people claim to follow me but instead follow the god of money and of fame and of majority rule. Today I invite you to pray earnestly for the strength that only I can provide to stand for my ways even when they come at a cost. And keep watch for the true followers I place in your life to support you. They will not be perfect any more than you are. Only I am perfect. But they can be your strength in the hardest of times.

January 25

1 Chronicles 1:1-7

• • •

Adam, Seth, Enosh; Kenan, Mahalalel, Jared; Enoch, Methuselah, Lamech; Noah, Shem, Ham, and Japheth. The descendants of Japheth: Gomer, Magog, Madai, Javan, Tubal, Meshech, and Tiras. The descendants of Gomer: Ashkenaz, Diphath, and Togarmah. The descendants of Javan: Elishah, Tarshish, Kittim, and Rodanim.

• • •

Imagine your entire nation being displaced and then finally getting to come back to the land your grandfather called home. Pretty disorienting. That's why my faithful child wrote Chronicles: to remind my beloved children that they had a legacy, despite the generations of disruption they had weathered. They needed the comfort of remembering they were descended from Adam, from Moses, from the prophets. They needed to know that they were a people—my people—even when life had torn them from the land they loved. Similarly, I want you to know that you are descended from Adam and Eve, from Moses and Miriam, from David and Jonathan and Ruth and Naomi. And you are an inheritor of their legacy of faithfulness and tenacity. You are my treasured child, made in my image as were they. Today I want you to look in a mirror and see where my image shines through your own image. And then I want you to reflect on how your whole faith community are inheritors of this legacy, that you stand on the shoulders of the judges and kings and prophets, called to a great calling for my sake, all made in my image.

January 26

1 Thessalonians 4:1

• • •

Finally, brothers and sisters, we ask and urge you in the Lord Jesus that, as you learned from us how you ought to live and to please God (as, in fact, you are doing), you should do so more and more.

• • •

None of my children but one has reached perfection. I know you and love you in your imperfections. But there is a saying popular in your generation, that I love you just the way you are and I love you too much to leave you that way. My son Paul's message to the church in Thessalonika 2,000 years ago is just as true for you and for your church today. I invite you to reflect on what you have learned about how to live in Christ, both as an individual and as a community. How will you strive to do so more and more?

January 27

2 Chronicles 5:13–14

• • •

it was the duty of the trumpeters and singers to make themselves heard in unison in praise and thanksgiving to the LORD, and when the song was raised, with trumpets and cymbals and other musical instruments, in praise to the LORD,
"For he is good,
for his steadfast love endures forever,"
the house, the house of the LORD, was filled with a cloud, so that the priests could not stand to minister because of the cloud; for the glory of the LORD filled the house of God.

• • •

I made you for joy and praise and celebration. I do not ask you to offer me thanksgiving because I need it. I ask you for it because sometimes you and your people have forgotten what joy feels like. You may even have forgotten that in an era such as this, when so much evil is afoot, celebration and thanksgiving are acts of resistance against evil forces, empires of destruction, and cultures of violence and hate. I love a good party because I love to see you shine with joy, and the world does not encourage joy for its own sake. Today I ask you to find something to celebrate, something to be thankful for, and to share it with someone. See if they can find something to celebrate and be thankful for as well. The trumpets and cymbals are optional, for today at least.

January 28

2 Thessalonians 1:3

• • •

We must always give thanks to God for you, brothers and sisters, as is right, because your faith is growing abundantly, and the love of every one of you for one another is increasing.

• • •

The author of the second letter to the church in Thessalonika was so proud of how they were being a community in Christ. When a spiritual community loves each other, really cares about each other, and helps each other to grow deeper in their love for me, nothing brings me greater joy. If all of those communities who professed to follow me were able to place love first, this world would be the world I dream of for you: a place where every need is met and every gift is honored, as I intended. Today I ask you to reflect on whether your faith community places love first, and how you would feel if it were able to do so even better. I made you for community...for a community like the one described in this text. You deserve that love.

January 29

Ezra 1:2-4

• • •

"Thus says King Cyrus of Persia: The LORD, the God of heaven, has given me all the kingdoms of the earth, and he has charged me to build him a house at Jerusalem in Judah. Any of those among you who are of his people—may their God be with them!—are now permitted to go up to Jerusalem in Judah, and rebuild the house of the LORD, the God of Israel—he is the God who is in Jerusalem; and let all survivors, in whatever place they reside, be assisted by the people of their place with silver and gold, with goods and with animals, besides freewill-offerings for the house of God in Jerusalem."

• • •

Do not limit whom I can work with and whom I can work through. King Cyrus was not Jewish. And yet he knew what I meant to my children of Israel. My son Cyrus let me work through him to build up my children of Israel after they had borne so much suffering in exile. Over and over I have worked with and through people who were not the expected vessels of my message. They have alleviated suffering and comforted and extended love in so many ways. It saddens me that my followers demonize so many people through whom I work. Today I invite you to reflect on the Cyruses in your own life who have brought you or those you know comfort, love, or access to dignity in some way. Lift them up in your prayers today, knowing that your God can turn so much to the good.

January 30

1 Timothy 1:15

• • •

The saying is sure and worthy of full acceptance, that Christ Jesus came into the world to save sinners—of whom I am the foremost.

• • •

I do not work through perfect people, as the author of this letter knew. And I have never known a sinner I did not love. I love you. I want your life to be a life of wholeness and fulfillment and millions of moments of joy. Know that you have done nothing that can separate you from me. Know that I long for your liberation and that I can offer compassion and forgiveness for anything...or even the same thing over and over until you are truly freed from it. Today I invite you to receive that compassion, to let go of something you want forgiveness for or do not think you deserve forgiveness for. And know that my love is enough to cover you. My Son came that you might be freed. Let him unlock the chains today that weigh you down.

January 31

Nehemiah 1:8–11

• • •

"Remember the word that you commanded your servant Moses, 'If you are unfaithful, I will scatter you among the peoples; but if you return to me and keep my commandments and do them, though your outcasts are under the farthest skies, I will gather them from there and bring them to the place at which I have chosen to establish my name.' They are your servants and your people, whom you redeemed by your great power and your strong hand. O Lord, let your ear be attentive to the prayer of your servant, and to the prayer of your servants who delight in revering your name. Give success to your servant today, and grant him mercy in the sight of this man!"

• • •

When my son Nehemiah prayed this prayer to me, the Israelites had done much to alienate themselves from me. They had broken trust with me over and over. They had abandoned me more times than you can count. Nehemiah came to me and confessed that he had fallen short of my glory and so had his family, and he entreated me to extend, once more, compassion to his people—my people. And I did. I listen when my children pray. I listen to every prayer you offer. I will never stop.

February

February 1

Esther 1:17b-18

• • •

"'King Ahasuerus commanded Queen Vashti to be brought before him, and she did not come.' This very day the noble ladies of Persia and Media who have heard of the queen's behavior will rebel against the king's officials, and there will be no end of contempt and wrath!"

• • •

When I think of the story of Queen Esther, my heart breaks, because the story could have turned out differently if my son Ahasuerus had realized that his wife Vashti was a human being of equal value to him. Great things happened in my name—great and terrible—because Esther took Vashti's place. But today I would like to invite you to reflect on the ways in which this world still treats some of my children as less than, while this world simultaneously makes them a source of terror. My son Ahasuerus was terrified that if he did not punish Vashti, women would rise up thinking they did not have to be constantly available to the whims of men. But it was my intent from the very beginning to make humanity—male and female—in my image. Remember that I treasure you as made in my image, whatever your gender. Remember I do not place any people above others. Today remember Vashti, risking so much to declare her full humanity and her *imago Dei*, her likeness to me. And pay attention to and honor the Vashti in you.

February 2

2 Timothy 1:6–7

• • •

For this reason I remind you to rekindle the gift of God that is within you through the laying on of my hands; for God did not give us a spirit of cowardice, but rather a spirit of power and of love and of self-discipline.

• • •

Whenever one of my beloved children transitions into another form of ministry in service to me, I love the way their faith family gathers around them and places hands on their head and shoulders and back as a sign of their sending the power of my love and light to that person to strengthen them for the task ahead. Today I invite you to think about the calling I have called you to, and I invite you to pause and feel my hand resting on your head, my power and my love coursing through you to strengthen you for the task. If there is someone in your life who needs a blessing, lay a hand on their head today and pray my love and power flow over them also. You deserve that strength. And when you have it in you, let it pour forth to others. That is how the power of my love keeps moving in the world.

February 3

Job 1:20-21

• • •

Then Job arose, tore his robe, shaved his head, and fell on the ground and worshiped. He said, "Naked I came from my mother's womb, and naked shall I return there; the LORD gave, and the LORD has taken away; blessed be the name of the LORD."

• • •

So many of my beloved children suffer because this world is full of injustice and the things that happen in the world feel so arbitrary. So many people blame other people for their own suffering, or they say I caused it. I want only your good. And so the story of my son Job is particularly precious to me because he endured so much and rejected those who told him it was because of his sin. He kept fighting for the right to be heard by me, and he remained faithful to me. I want my children to wrestle with and question injustice and to wrestle with me. I am strong enough to take it. Today I invite you to lift up a prayer to me about an injustice you face. Do not be afraid. I want your faithfulness. I do not want you to accept injustice or ever feel like you have to attribute your suffering to me.

February 4

Titus 1:7

• • •

For a bishop, as God's steward, must be blameless; he must not be arrogant or quick-tempered or addicted to wine or violent or greedy for gain.

• • •

Bishops are basically the pastors to the pastors. I want to make sure that the people who have dedicated their lives to me have a support system, since the best of them pour so much of themselves out for your sake and in my name. I am grateful for the saints who came before to remind the earliest bishops—and the bishops today—of the seriousness of this task. It makes me so sad when people abuse their power; it goes against my will and it damages your family. Today I invite you to pray for yourself as part of the priesthood of all believers, as well as for pastors and pastors-to-the-pastors, that my flock might know compassionate and good shepherds, so that my light and love might be shared with all in need without harm falling to a single sheep in my name.

February 5

Psalms 17:7–10

• • •

Wondrously show your steadfast love,
    O savior of those who seek refuge
    from their adversaries at your right hand.
Guard me as the apple of the eye;
    hide me in the shadow of your wings,
from the wicked who despoil me,
    my deadly enemies who surround me.
They close their hearts to pity;
    with their mouths they speak arrogantly.

• • •

Someone once said that the rest of the Bible is my love letter to you, humanity, and the book of Psalms is your love letter to me. One of the things that moves me about this love letter is how each psalm, whether it is praising me, petitioning me, or pleading with me, is so real and raw and vulnerable. Some psalms ask me to do violent things on someone's behalf. That is not how I intercede, but I want you to know that all of your emotions can find a safe place with me, that I am big enough to hold your heartbreak and your jubilance and your rage. I would rather you place them with me than misdirect them in harmful ways. Today I invite you to simply pray this passage to me, knowing that you *are* the apple of my eye and that like a mother bird I will hide you in the shelter of my wings, no matter what you are facing.

February 6

Philemon 1:3–5

• • •

Grace to you and peace from God our Father and the Lord Jesus Christ. When I remember you in my prayers, I always thank my God because I hear of your love for all the saints and your faith toward the Lord Jesus.

• • •

What a community can be built when you hold each other in love. I dream of a day when your whole community lifts you up as a saint and you hardly have enough hours in the day to celebrate all the saints who are blessing your life. Now, you know that even my saints aren't perfect, not one. But they strive hard to care for the world as a way of honoring me. I dream for you a full immersion into the community of saints, to be surrounded by that kind of love and commitment to me, to each other, and to the world that needs it so much. Today I invite you to offer up prayers of thanks for any saints in your life, and maybe let them know of your gratitude to them. You need solid support to live into your own sainthood.

February 7

Proverbs 1:20-22

• • •

Wisdom cries out in the street;
    in the squares she raises her voice.
At the busiest corner she cries out;
    at the entrance of the city gates she speaks:
"How long, O simple ones, will you love being simple?
How long will scoffers delight in their scoffing
    and fools hate knowledge?"

• • •

It is amazing how often I am right in the midst of people and they don't notice me. When I show up as wisdom in the feminine form, I am so often ignored. Even those who speak frequently of the Holy Spirit don't see me right in front of them, on the corner crying out to them, crying out for them to use reason and knowledge and the wisdom with which I bless them. Your generation shies away from truth as much as the generations before, to your own harm. So today I invite you to reflect on how you can connect yourself with greater knowledge, with greater wisdom. And I invite you to reflect on how to take greater care to recognize me in my many, many forms so that you may more easily turn to me and less easily shut me out.

February 8

Hebrews 2:16

• • •

For it is clear that he did not come to help angels, but the descendants of Abraham.

• • •

My Son did not come to earth to dwell among and honor the angels, the perfect, those without sin. Jesus came for you to thrive: you, my treasured creatures in all your imperfections, just as Abraham and his descendants were imperfect. Jesus came for you to reconnect to all of my sacred creation. So today I invite you to reflect on how I have shown up for your spiritual ancestors and how I might be showing up for you right now. And I invite you to let me in, to help, to heal, to comfort, to nudge you into who you were created to be.

February 9

Ecclesiastes 1:9–10

• • •

What has been is what will be,
    and what has been done is what will be done;
    there is nothing new under the sun.
Is there a thing of which it is said,
    "See, this is new"?
It has already been,
    in the ages before us.

• • •

Many people read this scripture and find it to be sad. I believe it can also be a word of comfort. You do not need to feel pressure to create anything brand new. You are welcome to focus your energies on living in my light, following in my ways, and seeking joy in doing good. The purpose of this life is not to win prizes for great new inventions (although if I have blessed you with gifts that will providing healing or comfort or a better life for people in need through your creativity or innovation, do not squander those gifts). The purpose of this life is to live right by me and to find joy in each other and in my creation. I invite you to explore where this message might be a word of hope in your own life, how it might free you from unfair expectations and open you up to my intentions for you.

February 10

James 1:2–4

• • •

My brothers and sisters, whenever you face trials of any kind, consider it nothing but joy, because you know that the testing of your faith produces endurance; and let endurance have its full effect, so that you may be mature and complete, lacking in nothing.

• • •

I do not want you to suffer. And yet I know that in this life there will be suffering. From the earliest days of my people Israel, and from the earliest days of the church, following my ways has resulted in suffering, because following me means rejecting the greed and violence and materialism and self-centeredness that this world fosters. And people who find a better path enrage those propping up the current system. So when you find that better path, when you choose to follow my ways, the world may seek to punish you as it has previous generations of faithful people. Do not be arrogant and boastful, and do not act as if you are being mistreated. Instead, reflect on how following me can help you meet some beautiful sojourners on this path with you, so that you do not have to journey alone, and that you are never alone when you are with me.

February 11

Isaiah 40:1–2

• • •

Comfort, O comfort my people,
   says your God.
Speak tenderly to Jerusalem,
   and cry to her
that she has served her term,
   that her penalty is paid,
that she has received from the LORD's hand
   double for all her sins.

• • •

It is true that when people sin, there are costs. My laws were intended to guide people to a better life for them and their community. When a nation sins, the costs of those sins multiply across many people. And yet what I always want is for reconciling and healing to occur, for things to be made right, for people to be able to get back on a path. Millenia ago, both religious and political leaders made sinful choices that put vulnerable people at risk. Their nation fell. And yet I did not abandon them. I dreamed of a day they would do right by me and be reconciled to me. And whenever anything you do creates a barrier between us, I pray the same for you, and for your nation also.

February 12

1 Peter 2:1–3

• • •

Rid yourselves, therefore, of all malice, and all guile, insincerity, envy, and all slander. Like newborn infants, long for the pure, spiritual milk, so that by it you may grow into salvation—if indeed you have tasted that the Lord is good.

• • •

I have a special love of babies, of their fragility and their unadulterated joy and their trust. Babies have an alive connection to me that I want to see in all of my children. Your generation sometimes values world weariness and even cynicism as badges of honor. And yet those things are barriers to your relationship with me. Today I invite you to consider how you might be a little more innocent in your relationship with me, a little less concerned about the world seeing you as gullible and a little more longing for us to grow closer.

February 13

Jeremiah 6:13-14

• • •

For from the least to the greatest of them,
everyone is greedy for unjust gain;
and from prophet to priest,
everyone deals falsely.
They have treated the wound of my people carelessly,
saying, "Peace, peace,"
when there is no peace.

• • •

Someday you will find a way to honor each other and recognize that the land does not belong to you but you belong to the land. And there will be peace. And yet from generation to generation, people place fear of each other and fear of not having enough (and greed for more than they need) ahead of their relationship with me. It is true of your generation also. Jeremiah was a faithful prophet who reminded his people of this. Can I call on you to be my prophet for peace? Today I invite you to reflect on your role in naming how people need to place each other before their own needs in order to truly be my people.

February 14

2 Peter 1:3

• • •

His divine power has given us everything needed for life and godliness, through the knowledge of him who called us by his own glory and goodness.

• • •

I have made sure there is enough for all of you, and for those of you who follow my Son to have all the resources needed for a beautiful life together. My Son set out a model of how to live that creates abundance and highlights simplicity as a means of being closer to me. Today I invite you to reflect on what you know about my Son and his goodness, and how you can apply those lessons to the way you live in community.

February 15

Lamentations 1:1

• • •

How lonely sits the city
    that once was full of people!
How like a widow she has become,
    she that was great among the nations!
She that was a princess among the provinces
    has become a vassal.

• • •

This world sees grief as weakness. But I have watched people suffer needlessly because they did not acknowledge the grief they carried. There is a whole book of the Bible that shows you how to grieve without restraint, to pour out your pain at my feet, to name all of your sense of loss. In Lamentations, the writer grieved all that Israel lost and endured in war and in exile before reconciling with me and returning home. Today I ask you to reflect on what rituals of grief you need to engage in, alone or with others, to experience release of the pain you carry, so that you and I can grow closer. Know that I can hold all of your pain, but only if you are willing to set it down.

February 16

1 John 1:8-10

• • •

If we say that we have no sin, we deceive ourselves, and the truth is not in us. If we confess our sins, he who is faithful and just will forgive us our sins and cleanse us from all unrighteousness. If we say that we have not sinned, we make him a liar, and his word is not in us.

• • •

One of the biggest barriers my children face to being in relationship with me isn't sin: it's your inability to admit your sin. My Son once famously called on you to forgive, not seven times but seven times seventy, and how much more generous am I? But in order to heal from your stumbles and shortcomings, the times you were unkind or participated in injustice, you need to name them and earnestly desire to turn away from them. Today I invite you to explore what shortcoming you would like to be healed from. Offer it up to me, and I will forgive it. And find a friend who can help you seek a new way of living.

February 17

Ezekiel 16:49

• • •

This was the guilt of your sister Sodom: she and her daughters had pride, excess of food, and prosperous ease, but did not aid the poor and needy.

• • •

I created an earth with so much bounty, so much for everyone as long as you were generous with each other. And yet from the earliest days of my creation, people have been consumed by fear and greed. People have twisted my will and blamed poor people for their poverty instead of helping them out of poverty. Today I invite you to reflect on where you witness this withholding in your own community and what response you and I can create with others who follow my will that all of my children be clothed and nourished and cared for.

February 18

2 John 1:3

• • •

Grace, mercy, and peace will be with us from God the Father and from Jesus Christ, the Father's Son, in truth and love.

• • •

It takes so little for us to be close. Whenever you extend love, we grow closer. Whenever you live your life with integrity, I am there with you. It is my deepest longing that you and all my creation could feel my grace, mercy, and peace. I feel all the ways you seek me. Know that I am there, embracing you. Know that I celebrate all the ways in which you share my love with those around you. Today I invite you to notice all the small kindnesses you do, and recognize my presence with you as you spread my love.

February 19

Daniel 3:16–18

• • •

Shadrach, Meshach, and Abednego answered the king, "O Nebuchadnezzar, we have no need to present a defense to you in this matter. If our God whom we serve is able to deliver us from the furnace of blazing fire and out of your hand, O king, let him deliver us. But if not, be it known to you, O king, that we will not serve your gods and we will not worship the golden statue that you have set up."

• • •

The story of my faithful servants Shadrach, Meshach, and Abednego has been famous for many years. People tend to focus on the miracle of how they survived the fiery furnace that the king had placed them in. But I want you to pay attention to something else: they were put in the furnace for refusing to worship anyone but me. They willingly took the risk of death, not knowing whether they would survive, in order to be faithful to me. What are the things that distract you from honoring me? What are the gods that those in power ask you to worship? How might you model for others a way to resist those gods?

February 20

3 John 1:3-4

• • •

I was overjoyed when some of the friends arrived and testified to your faithfulness to the truth, namely how you walk in the truth. I have no greater joy than this, to hear that my children are walking in the truth.

• • •

If an apostle's friends had been witness to your community life, what would they report back to the apostle? Or if they were witness to your personal life, what would their word be? The apostle wrote this letter to a man named Gaius to get him and his community ready for the visit of another beloved apostle named Demetrius, and the author was relieved to find that Demetrius would be working with good and open people. Today I invite you to ask how you and your community are readying yourself for the apostles I send to you to strengthen you. How are you practicing hospitality, transparency, and visible faithfulness to me and my message of love? How can you support each other in those practices?

FEB
Liberating Love

February 21

Hosea 5:14b–15

• • •

I myself will tear and go away;
　I will carry off, and no one shall rescue.
I will return again to my place
　until they acknowledge their guilt and seek my face.
　In their distress they will beg my favor.

• • •

Throughout ancient times, I would call on prophets to let my people know that I would not aid them in their wrongdoing. In the time of Hosea, I let the people know that they would not be able to communicate with me until they faced their wrongdoing and repented. The same remains true today. I will love your community into a new way of being, but I will not love its sin, and I will not linger to make you think I am supporting it. The role of the prophet is hard, to bring to the people my word that they need to realign with me in order to thrive. Some are called to prophesy to the community, and some to help the community turn back to me. Today I invite you to reflect on your role.

February 22

Jude 1:20

• • •

But you, beloved, build yourselves up
on your most holy faith; pray in the Holy Spirit.

• • •

My spirit is known by so many names: *Ruach* in the Hebrew, meaning breath. Lady Wisdom, so much ignored in the book of Proverbs. And the one most commonly used by followers of my Son Jesus: the Holy Spirit, who intercedes with sighs too deep for words when you cannot give language to your prayers. The power of the Spirit is not that it moves when your faith is unbreakable, but when you feel absolutely broken apart. Your most holy faith is not the same thing as certainty, and the Spirit is there to support you and to pray wordless prayers with you and nudge you and call to you and embrace you when you feel absolutely uncertain. How can you let in my Spirit today? Where can she show up in you and for you today?

February 23

Joel 2:12–13

• • •

Yet even now, says the LORD,
   return to me with all your heart,
with fasting, with weeping, and with mourning;
   rend your hearts and not your clothing.
Return to the LORD, your God,
   for he is gracious and merciful,
slow to anger, and abounding in steadfast love,
   and relents from punishing.

• • •

You may notice how many of the passages in the ancient scriptures are not focused on the actions of individuals but on the collective actions of a whole people. There is a strange trend in recent generations to focus on the individual. And I love you deeply; I made you unique. But my will is not for you to be good individuals. My will is for you to be a good people. My prophet Joel invited my people to rend their hearts—make themselves vulnerable—so that I could embrace them and guide them rather than punish them. That is my will for your community also, however small. How can I heal what is hurting in your community today? Invite me in, and invite others into your prayer.

February 24

Revelation 2:4–5a

• • •

But I have this against you, that you have abandoned the love you had at first. Remember then from what you have fallen; repent, and do the works you did at first.

• • •

The book of Revelation is one of the most widely misunderstood of your sacred texts. What is most important for you is my messages to the churches that existed at the time. This message was to the church in Ephesus. They did good works and cast out false prophets. They did not tolerate lies. But they had forgotten the *why* of the laws I had given them: I wanted them to live in love. Love is *always* the why behind my words and guidance and laws. How can you reground your actions in love today, for my sake and for yours?

February 25

Amos 2:11-12

• • •

And I raised up some of your children to be prophets
  and some of your youths to be nazirites.
Is it not indeed so, O people of Israel?
says the Lord.
But you made the nazirites drink wine,
  and commanded the prophets,
  saying, "You shall not prophesy."

• • •

So often my people forget my purpose, sometimes as soon as a single generation. When my prophet Amos brought my strong indictment of my children Israel, they had forgotten to honor the prophets and priests I had placed in their midst. Instead they did harm to prophets and corrupted priests. Part of how they let this happen is that my children forgot that they were connected to me and to each other. When you know each other to be family, you care for each other and prop each other up. Sometimes people resent those in your midst who bring you a hard word to help you be your best selves. Who are those people in your community today? Their job can be difficult and lonely, and they are there for your thriving. How can you honor and support them?

February 26

Matthew 3:1-3

• • •

In those days John the Baptist appeared in the wilderness of Judea, proclaiming, "Repent, for the kingdom of heaven has come near." This is the one of whom the prophet Isaiah spoke when he said,

"The voice of one crying out in the wilderness:
'Prepare the way of the Lord,
    make his paths straight.'"

• • •

Sometimes the English translation loses what was intended by my earlier prophets who spoke Hebrew and Aramaic. The kingdom of heaven has come near. The kingdom of heaven is at hand. *The kingdom of heaven is within you*. What might it mean for you, my beloved child, if my treasured son John the Baptist was trying to let you know that my realm, my reign, can be accessed not geographically, not beyond the grave, but within yourself? What does my realm look like and feel like? Today I invite you to reflect on the ways you have embodied my realm here on earth, and to honor that. Consider asking others to do the same and imagine how you can do that more and more.

February 27

Obadiah 1:3-4

• • •

Your proud heart has deceived you,
    you that live in the clefts of the rock,
    whose dwelling is in the heights.
You say in your heart,
    "Who will bring me down to the ground?"
Though you soar aloft like the eagle,
    though your nest is set among the stars,
    from there I will bring you down,
                says the LORD.

• • •

There is hardly a book in your sacred texts that does not call you to a life of humility. The best kings of Israel were humble, and when they failed to be humble their realms fell. This world punishes humility, but my realm rewards it beyond measure. A community grounded in humility is so much stronger and less prone to destruction from inside or out. I do not call you to humility only because it is right, but also because it is the only way to truly thrive. But humility requires a level of confidence in one's own value that the braggarts and loud bullies who lead nations today simply do not possess. Today reflect on what it means to be a treasured child of mine. Reflect on how much I love you. Reflect on what that makes possible. It is the beginning of the path to true spiritual humility.

February 28

Mark 3:31–35

• • •

Then his mother and his brothers came; and standing outside, they sent to him and called him. A crowd was sitting around him; and they said to him, "Your mother and your brothers and sisters are outside, asking for you." And he replied, "Who are my mother and my brothers?" And looking at those who sat around him, he said, "Here are my mother and my brothers! Whoever does the will of God is my brother and sister and mother."

• • •

You have heard the phrase "blood is thicker than water." My Son rejected this statement outright. When you follow me, you are the brother and sister and mother of Jesus. When you follow me, you have a family of a completely different type than that formed by biology. Jesus claims you as part of his family. How will you likewise claim him? How will you do my will and build up relationships with your holy family today?

February 29

Jonah 1:1-3

• • •

Now the word of the LORD came to Jonah son of Amittai, saying, "Go at once to Nineveh, that great city, and cry out against it; for their wickedness has come up before me." ³But Jonah set out to flee to Tarshish from the presence of the LORD He went down to Joppa and found a ship going to Tarshish; so he paid his fare and went on board, to go with them to Tarshish, away from the presence of the LORD.

• • •

I have so much love for my faithful and resentful servant Jonah. He reminds me of you. He knew what my will was, but he also knew that I was compassionate, and I had asked him to give a people he hated one more chance at redemption. He did not want them redeemed. He did not think they deserved to be redeemed. And so he turned away from the task I had given him. You already know what happened next, but today I want you to extend some sympathy to your brother Jonah. I want you to think about times you have turned away from the task I called you to, knowing it was right but not being ready to accept it. And I invite you to consider accepting that task, even knowing that my mercy is often not palatable to this world of retribution.

March

March 1

Micah 3:5

• • •

Thus says the LORD concerning the prophets
    who lead my people astray,
who cry "Peace"
    when they have something to eat,
but declare war against those
    who put nothing into their mouths.

• • •

There is usually an arc to the truth-telling of my prophets: "You are doing wrong by God in this way; here is the horror about to befall you because you defy God. However, if you turn back to God, here are the wonders God will create, because God loves you." My son Micah pointed to false prophets who focused only on themselves. Today consider who helps guide you with no concern for their personal gain. Lift up my real prophets with gratitude today.

March 2

Luke 5:30–32

• • •

The Pharisees and their scribes were complaining to his disciples, saying, "Why do you eat and drink with tax collectors and sinners?" Jesus answered, "Those who are well have no need of a physician, but those who are sick; I have come to call not the righteous but sinners to repentance."

• • •

Judgment devoid of compassion or possibility of reconciliation has never been my way. That didn't change when my Son came to earth. He came to those who needed him and to those open to receiving him. Sometimes the people who see themselves as most righteous are the ones most likely to miss out on my presence. In fact, they didn't realize they were missing out on spending time with my Son because they were so busy worrying about who else he spent time with. Today I invite you to reflect on how you might be a little less righteous and a little more open to where I show up, so that we can be together even more.

March 3

Nahum 1:7-8a

• • •

The LORD is good,
    a stronghold in a day of trouble;
he protects those who take refuge in him,
    even in a rushing flood.

• • •

This world is a hard and scary place. Rushing floods are real. Days of trouble are real. And I always commit to being with you in the midst of challenge. There is a story of a man in a flood who prayed to me to save him. He rejected help from people in a car driving by as the waters rose, and then a boat, and then a helicopter. He drowned and went to heaven and asked why I wasn't there to save him. "What was wrong with the car and boat and helicopter?" I responded. It's not a factual story, but it's a true story. I work actively through my children. Today I ask you to reflect on how my support is available to you through my children on earth with you now.

March 4

John 3:8

• • •

"The wind blows where it chooses, and you hear the sound of it, but you do not know where it comes from or where it goes. So it is with everyone who is born of the Spirit."

• • •

My love is for your liberation. When you are truly in me, you are completely free. You belong to the world, and you can also hear where in the world you are needed. When my Son spoke these words, he invited you into a giddy-making and freedom-making journey, untethered by the judgment of the world or the rules of the world that were not created for your joy. Today I ask you to imagine what it would feel like to be as free as the wind, and ponder whether you are ready to join my Son and the Holy Spirit in that journey. Then I ask you to seek my help in becoming fully free.

March 5

Habakkuk 1:2–4

• • •

O LORD, how long shall I cry for help,
    and you will not listen?
Or cry to you "Violence!"
    and you will not save?
Why do you make me see wrongdoing
    and look at trouble?
Destruction and violence are before me;
    strife and contention arise.
So the law becomes slack
    and justice never prevails.
The wicked surround the righteous—
    therefore judgment comes forth perverted.

• • •

The thing about my prophets is how much they love me, and how much they love my people. When my servant Habakkuk called out to me like this, he was pained by the injustice and violence to which he was witness. He wished he could turn away. What blesses me about him is that he ultimately knew he couldn't, if he wanted his people to be free from evil and injustice. He needed to bring my word to them (and particularly their leaders who were responsible for so much injustice) for the sake of his people's redemption and liberation, so that his people would know true peace. Today I ask you to reflect on where violence is in your community and whether you feel the same heartbreak as my prophets did, and what I might be calling you to do in response.

March 6

Acts 4:13

• • •

Now when they saw the boldness of Peter and John and realized that they were uneducated and ordinary men, they were amazed and recognized them as companions of Jesus.

• • •

My most faithful followers have sometimes been geniuses, and sometimes they have been average. Some of them have been legendarily noble and moral, and some of them have had a shady past...some struggle to do right even after they have committed themselves to me. Some have been kings and some have been sex workers. What matters to me about my followers is that their hearts long for relationship with me and they are boldly, unapologetically seeking to do my will, even when they fail. You are part of a long legacy of faithful servants, and I hope you feel them supporting and encouraging you. Today I invite you to pray for the boldness of Peter and John, knowing you are just as worthy, and just as chosen, and just as needed for your time as they were for theirs. You are a true companion of Jesus and I want the world to recognize you as such.

March 7

Zephaniah 1:7–9

• • •

Be silent before the Lord God!
    For the day of the Lord is at hand;
the Lord has prepared a sacrifice,
    he has consecrated his guests.
And on the day of the Lord's sacrifice
I will punish the officials and the king's sons
    and all who dress themselves in foreign attire.
On that day I will punish
    all who leap over the threshold,
who fill their master's house
    with violence and fraud.

• • •

Almost every one of my prophets has warned of the consequences of rejecting my will. Zephaniah was no exception, and he brought my word faithfully to the people. He warned them that those who deny and forget me, who are seduced by the glamour of other nations, will suffer from their broken relationship with me. Harm to my people and exploitation of my people—violence and fraud—those are things I loathe. Today I invite you to reflect on where you are witness to, and where you are called to speak out against, violence and fraud in your midst, for the sake of my most vulnerable children.

March 8

Romans 3:27-28

• • •

Then what becomes of boasting? It is excluded. By what law? By that of works? No, but by the law of faith. For we hold that a person is justified by faith apart from works prescribed by the law.

• • •

Hundreds of years ago there were pitched battles between different groups of my followers about which matters most: faith or works? The answer remains now what it was then and what it was in the days after my Son ascended to heaven. I am a God of compassion who values most your faith in me and your repentance of sin. And when you have truly repented and truly sought to live in my will, you will not be able to help but engage in good works out of a desire for everyone to experience the love that you know. Today I invite you to reflect on how your actions mirror your relationship with me. And I invite you to pray for support in living out your joy in me in all the ways you can.

March 9

Haggai 1:7–8

• • •

Thus says the LORD of hosts: Consider how you have fared. Go up to the hills and bring wood and build the house, so that I may take pleasure in it and be honored, says the LORD.

• • •

Some of my followers have pointed out that the prophets aren't so much warning that I will destroy those who don't follow me, but instead making it clear that straying from my ways brings inevitable consequences, the same way that eating only meat and no vegetables leads to bad health without any intervention on my part. In the days of the prophet Haggai, the people had placed their wants before honoring me; my temple was a ruin while some of them lived large. Haggai pointed out that things had not gone well for them when they strayed from me and now it was time to put me first, for their sake more than mine. Today I ask you to reflect on what your community values more than their relationship with me, and the ways in which they have neglected me, and what your role could be in helping them so that they may live a fuller life.

March 10

1 Corinthians 4:1–2

• • •

Think of us in this way, as servants of Christ and stewards of God's mysteries. Moreover, it is required of stewards that they should be found trustworthy.

• • •

Steward is no romantic term. The English term comes from sty-ward, the servants who cared for cattle or pigs. It is not a glamorous position, but it is an essential one. Today I want you to reflect on what it means that I trust you, and believe you to be so glorious that you do not need to hold a glamorous position to know your worth. Know that I trust you to hold and to share the mystery of my love with all those in need. Know that you are worthy of the task of serving with my Son Jesus.

March 11

Zechariah 1:3-4

. . .

Therefore say to them, Thus says the LORD of hosts: Return to me, says the LORD of hosts, and I will return to you, says the LORD of hosts. Do not be like your ancestors, to whom the former prophets proclaimed, "Thus says the LORD of hosts, Return from your evil ways and from your evil deeds." But they did not hear or heed me, says the LORD.

. . .

Many of my children have been given countless opportunities to return to me. Whole generations have ignored that plea to their detriment. When my children fell away, their nation unraveled through in–fighting and the loss of the spiritual practices that held them together, as other influences crept in. Generations ended up in exile when their nation fell. Zechariah came to remind them it was still not too late to reconnect with me. You have been given the same chance: connect with me now. Hear me. Heed me. And help your community stay rooted in my ways. Today I invite you to reflect on your journey and what it has felt like, or would feel like, to return to me. Give thanks and pray.

March 12

2 Corinthians 4:7-10

• • •

But we have this treasure in clay jars, so that it may be made clear that this extraordinary power belongs to God and does not come from us. We are afflicted in every way, but not crushed; perplexed, but not driven to despair; persecuted, but not forsaken; struck down, but not destroyed; always carrying in the body the death of Jesus, so that the life of Jesus may also be made visible in our bodies.

• • •

Human life is fragile, and the life of a real follower carries its own burdens. When we practice generosity and vulnerability and abundant love, some people will seek to exploit or deride or crush those things. That is why I made you for community, so that you would not have to bear these burdens alone. It is why from the days Paul wrote this letter of encouragement to the Jesus followers in Corinth, I have called people to build up a community so that you would not be crushed or driven to despair or feel forsaken or destroyed, because you would be able to bear these burdens together. The scripture describes the Holy Spirit as a Paraclete, an advocate. And the Holy Spirit resides in you. Today give thanks for the paracletes—the encouragers—who bring my children together and offer comfort and strength and hope in these hard times. Honor your own fragility and your own beauty—you are a clay jar. And you hold treasure beyond reckoning.

March 13

Malachi 1:10a

• • •

O that someone among you would shut the temple doors, so that you would not kindle fire on my altar in vain!

• • •

In that ancient debate over faith versus works, my servant Malachi reminded my people that I do not want you worshiping with empty hearts, out of obligation. If your worship is not authentic, that worship is an offense to me. Malachi sent my word to my people that it would be better if they didn't go into the temple at all, because it was all empty ritual. I know that sometimes you go to worship without wanting to be there because you hope it will bring you a lift, and that is great. My concern is with a whole community that is simply going through the motions. Today I invite you to reflect on the depth and passion of your community's worship to me and how you might help stoke or rekindle an authentic flame in their midst.

March 14

Galatians 1:10

• • •

Am I now seeking human approval, or God's approval? Or am I trying to please people? If I were still pleasing people, I would not be a servant of Christ.

• • •

It is the human condition to want to be liked. For many of my children, it was how you survived a hard childhood or protected yourself from harm. And you hold onto those learned behaviors for many years, wanting to be safe. My child, today I invite you to reflect on what it means to put your trust in my Son, who will never betray you, even more than you place trust in the people around you. I want you to live as your fully authentic self, which builds a richer and more meaningful connection to the people you need in your life than being a people pleaser could ever offer.

March 15

Genesis 18:1–3

• • •

The LORD appeared to Abraham by the oaks of Mamre, as he sat at the entrance of his tent in the heat of the day. He looked up and saw three men standing near him. When he saw them, he ran from the tent entrance to meet them, and bowed down to the ground. He said, "My lord, if I find favor with you, do not pass by your servant."

• • •

Something that was taught and practiced by my earliest followers is a culture of hospitality. Welcoming the stranger is one of the most reverent acts you can perform. Abraham did not know that the men he greeted were angels sent by me. What he knew is that human beings are created in my image, and that the starting place of all encounters should be one of generosity. Welcoming the friend is easy. Welcoming family is easy...depending on the family. But welcoming the stranger is not about their relationship to you. It is about you knowing their relationship to me: one of my beloved children. Today I invite you to reflect on the ways you have extended kindness to strangers in the past, and I invite you to wonder what it would feel like to extend that kindness even further, letting the person you greet know that you see in them my image.

March 16

Ephesians 2:17–19

• • •

So he came and proclaimed peace to you who were far off and peace to those who were near; for through him both of us have access in one Spirit to the Father. So then you are no longer strangers and aliens, but you are citizens with the saints and also members of the household of God.

• • •

My most enlightened followers have learned this: there is no "us" and "them." There is only us. You are part of one large family that transcends all of the manmade geographical boundaries. I made you one family. It was humanity that created dividing walls. The early followers in Jerusalem and Rome and Ephesus had access to Christ despite what were in those days vast geographic divides. They were equally siblings in my Son, the Prince of Peace. You now span the globe. So who are the strangers and aliens? There are none. You are fully embraced as my child. So are all your brothers and sisters. When you all learn to live this, there will be peace.

March 17

Exodus 3:11–12

• • •

But Moses said to God, "Who am I that I should go to Pharaoh, and bring the Israelites out of Egypt?" He said, "I will be with you; and this shall be the sign for you that it is I who sent you: when you have brought the people out of Egypt, you shall worship God on this mountain."

• • •

Whenever you feel inadequate for the task to which I have called you (and you can usually tell it's from me because it's something you feel inadequate to do), remember my treasured son Moses. He had a bundle of excuses, and yet I made sure he had my support. I also sent his brother Aaron with him for encouragement and strength. Two-by-two is a better way to bring my word when you can, because when you're telling Pharaoh to free the people he has enslaved, it's daunting work. Whatever excuses you have, know that I will only give you the task you are equipped for, and in your midst is likely to be the partner to support you. Consider your task. List the reasons you can't do it. And ask if I can't help you overcome them.

March 18

Philippians 2:1–2

• • •

If then there is any encouragement in Christ, any consolation from love, any sharing in the Spirit, any compassion and sympathy, make my joy complete: be of the same mind, having the same love, being in full accord and of one mind.

• • •

What Paul asks of the church in Philippi is no easy task. He asks it with love because he cares for them so much, and he knows it will help them grow in their support of each other and their relationship with me. But it is heartbreakingly rare that my followers are able to engage the level of humility necessary to find any sort of unity around how to be my people together. And so today I invite you simply to pray for the church, that it would be a place for people to escape the conflict and dissent sown in the world, and a place of compassion. For that is the secret, my child: an abundance of compassion, not an abundance of facts, is what leads to being of one mind in Christ.

March 19

Leviticus 19:33–34

• • •

When an alien resides with you in your land, you shall not oppress the alien. The alien who resides with you shall be to you as the citizen among you; you shall love the alien as yourself, for you were aliens in the land of Egypt: I am the LORD your God.

• • •

Even when you have had an experience, you forget. Even when you have had an experience, your children may not understand it. That is why over and over I made sure to remind my children of their history, so that it could influence the way they lived in the present day. And so today I remind you also: your spiritual ancestors were foreigners who ended up in Egypt. How might you care for the foreigners among you now? It has been part of what it meant to follow me from the time of Abram to today.

March 20

Colossians 2:2-3

• • •

I want their hearts to be encouraged and united in love, so that they may have all the riches of assured understanding and have the knowledge of God's mystery, that is, Christ himself, in whom are hidden all the treasures of wisdom and knowledge.

• • •

The author of the letter to the church in Colossae wanted people who had never met him to feel encouraged and connected to Jesus Christ. Likewise it is my longing that you connect to my Son, the source of wisdom and knowledge. My love is greater than you can comprehend and bigger than anything you can imagine. But through my Son you can get a glimpse of how big love can be. Today think of the mysteries you want to unravel. Turn to Jesus and ask him to point you toward the answers you seek for the sake of doing my will.

March 21

Numbers 8:23–25

• • •

The LORD spoke to Moses, saying: This applies to the Levites: from twenty-five years old and upwards they shall begin to do duty in the service of the tent of meeting; and from the age of fifty years they shall retire from the duty of the service and serve no more.

• • •

Another sacred book points out that to everything there is a season. Those serving in my house were called to service for a specific number of years because people are called to different roles during different seasons of their lives. In your younger years, I may need your passion and outrage at injustice. In your middle years, I might need your thoughtfulness and diplomacy and community-building gifts. In your later years I will need you to bring the wisdom and humility and spiritual grounding of an elder. Reflect today on what season you are in, what I called you to at different seasons, and what I call you to in this season.

March 22

1 Thessalonians 4:9

• • •

Now concerning love of the brothers and sisters, you do not need to have anyone write to you, for you yourselves have been taught by God to love one another.

• • •

It is my simplest and most frequently violated law: Love one another. Simple is not the same as easy. And so today I invite you into a particular prayer practice: pray to me that you might know peace and love and abundance. Then pray the same for family members (by name, including the ones you don't like). Then for your friends. Then for your neighbors. Then for the people you don't like. Then pray for local, then state, then national leaders, by name. Last, pray for the whole world, people and creation alike.

March 23

Deuteronomy 1:31

• • •

...and in the wilderness, where you saw how the LORD your God carried you, just as one carries a child, all the way that you traveled until you reached this place.

• • •

There is a popular poem called "Footprints." It actually harks back to an ancient message from the sacred texts. For tens of thousands of years, when your ancestors faced their hardest times, I carried them. During your hardest times, I carry you with the love that a mom, a dad, an aunty or uncle might take, gently holding you throughout the journey. And I will continue to carry you and your whole community just as I carried all of Israel out of bondage and into liberation. My arms are that big and my love is that great. Today simply imagine me carrying you and all of your people into a better place. Pray me into that journey with you.

March 24

2 Thessalonians 1:11–12

• • •

To this end we always pray for you, asking that our God will make you worthy of his call and will fulfill by his power every good resolve and work of faith, so that the name of our Lord Jesus may be glorified in you, and you in him, according to the grace of our God and the Lord Jesus Christ.

• • •

You are my hands and feet in the world, as my beloved daughter St. Teresa of Ávila famously said, My Son has no hands or feet on earth but yours. And I am always here to work through you, because it is through your love and compassion and generosity that people encounter me. Every time you seek to do something kind today, imagine me bolstering you, supporting you. Imagine people who need me getting to experience me through you, and their hearts being a little more whole as a result. I am so glad you are my ambassador today.

March 25

Joshua 6:18

• • •

As for you, keep away from the things devoted to destruction, so as not to covet and take any of the devoted things and make the camp of Israel an object for destruction, bringing trouble upon it.

• • •

"Beware the company you keep" is a saying popular not so long ago, and it is worth considering. It is important to stay in relationship with people who need you. It is important, though, to create distance from those who do not seek for you to thrive and grow closer to me. This is true for you and it is true for your community. How are you making sure that you build a community devoted to strengthening my work of love, not a community prone to gossip and power grabbing and judgment? How can I be ever more a part of that process?

March 26

1 Timothy 3:16b

• • •

He was revealed in flesh,
    vindicated in spirit,
    seen by angels,
proclaimed among Gentiles,
    believed in throughout the world,
        taken up in glory.

• • •

My beloved Son was divine and human. He understood all the challenges you face, and he was in constant connection with me. That remains true today. And also, my beloved child, he was meant to be a model for you, because I was not lying when in the beginning I said I would make you in my image. You are fully human, and you have the touch of the divine on you. As you follow my Son, you too will be vindicated in spirit and when your work on this earth is through, you will be taken up in glory. Today I simply invite you to sit in awe of that reality, in awe of who you are.

March 27

Judges 6:7–10

• • •

When the Israelites cried to the LORD on account of the
Midianites, the LORD sent a prophet to the Israelites; and he
said to them, "Thus says the LORD, the God of Israel: I led you
up from Egypt, and brought you out of the house of slavery; and
I delivered you from the hand of the Egyptians, and from the
hand of all who oppressed you, and drove them out before you,
and gave you their land; and I said to you, 'I am the LORD your
God; you shall not pay reverence to the gods of the Amorites, in
whose land you live.' But you have not given heed to my voice."

• • •

Sometimes I am described as a jealous God. What I
seek, though, is for you to follow a path of love and
faithfulness, because that is as intricately connected to
liberation as my leading you out of Egypt. When you worship
the gods of the lands around you, you also adopt practices
that are in opposition to my way of love and faithfulness.
Follow me and stay free. Today I invite you to think about
the gods in the land where you live, and how to stay free
of them.

March 28

2 Timothy 1:8–9a

• • •

Do not be ashamed, then, of the testimony about our Lord or of me his prisoner, but join with me in suffering for the gospel, relying on the power of God, who saved us and called us with a holy calling, not according to our works but according to his own purpose and grace.

• • •

In the earliest years after my Son's ascension into heaven, people thought it scandalous that anyone would worship a common criminal. When his earliest followers stood up against Rome's expectation that all Roman citizens treat Caesar as a god, they were jailed too, adding to the scandal of this new path to me. Your generation still treats those in prison with shame or embarrassment, and yet many of my most faithful servants are behind bars. How is your community supporting them when they return home? How are you making use of their gifts and supporting their calling? I am no more ashamed of them than I am of my own Son. I invite you to reflect on how you can embrace them too.

March 29

Ruth 1:20b–21

• • •

"Call me no longer Naomi,
　　call me Mara,
　　　for the Almighty has dealt bitterly with me.
I went away full,
　　but the Lord has brought me back empty;
why call me Naomi
　　when the Lord has dealt harshly with me,
　　and the Almighty has brought calamity upon me?"

• • •

You have heard me say this before, but I am strong enough to hold all your pain, all your heartbreak, all your rage, all your sorrow. When my beloved daughter Naomi lost both of her sons as well as her husband, she felt abandoned and alone. She told her friends she had changed her name to that of a bitter herb, to reflect on how badly I had treated her. My love for her did not falter. I knew that she had a daughter-in-law, Ruth, who would be her lifeline during a horrible time and would go on to be a critical part of the lineage of Israel. Today, know that no matter what you are feeling, I can hold it. I love you. I am big enough to take anything you need to throw at me, and I will be here when you have nothing left to throw, to hold you and support you.

March 30

Titus 1:8

• • •

...but [a bishop] must be hospitable, a lover of goodness, prudent, upright, devout, and self-controlled.

• • •

Again, bishops are simply pastors-to-the pastors, the people who support those called to the particular calling of shepherding my people as you each grow fully into your roles in the priesthood of all believers. If you know people in your life with these spiritual gifts, or if you have these spiritual gifts, seek ways to make sure that my shepherds are being supported so that they serve your community (which is also my community) in the ways you need and I intend. In that way, you all pastor each other.

March 31

1 Samuel 3:8–9

• • •

The LORD called Samuel again, a third time. And he got up and went to Eli, and said, "Here I am, for you called me." Then Eli perceived that the LORD was calling the boy. Therefore Eli said to Samuel, "Go, lie down; and if he calls you, you shall say, 'Speak, LORD, for your servant is listening.'" So Samuel went and lay down in his place.

• • •

Have you ever heard words of wisdom or instruction or guidance from three different people back-to-back? That may have been me. I speak to my children in many ways, the ways best suited to them, if they are listening. Some people hear me through a whispered word. Some hear me through mentors. Some hear me through strangers. Some hear me directly through prayer. And some hear me through the pages of scripture. When was the last time you heard something and wondered if it might be from me? Today I invite you to sit with how you listen best and consider how I might be trying to reach you today.

April

APR · Liberating Love

365 LOVE NOTES FROM GOD

April 1

2 Samuel 5:12

• • •

David then perceived that the LORD had established him king over Israel, and that he had exalted his kingdom for the sake of his people Israel.

• • •

My son Saul fell away from my path and my son David stepped into his place. Part of the reason David's time as king began well was because he knew that his role was to care for his people Israel. Whenever he lost sight of that, things went really wrong. This is true for you, too, even if you are not a king. You will know greater harmony when you are serving and acting for the sake of my people than when you are seeking only your own gain. You have the power to affect the lives of my beloved children around you. I trust you with that power. Today I ask you to reflect on the power you have as my faithful servant and how to wield it well for my sake.

April 2

Philemon 1:6

• • •

I pray that the sharing of your faith may become effective when you perceive all the good that we may do for Christ.

• • •

Sometimes even the most faithful of you can feel a little defeated. The letter to Philemon was a reminder that your work is not in vain, that any good acts you do make a big difference for the sake of witnessing to Jesus' love for his siblings. Be encouraged, my beloved child. Your compassion and generosity are making the world a better place at a time when many are trying to sow fear and hatred and greed, the opposite of Jesus' message. I see you. I see the love you share. It is powerful. Today I invite you to let me in to celebrate all the good in you.

April 3

1 Kings 3:7–9

• • •

"And now, O Lᴏʀᴅ my God, you have made your servant king in place of my father David, although I am only a little child; I do not know how to go out or come in. And your servant is in the midst of the people whom you have chosen, a great people, so numerous they cannot be numbered or counted. Give your servant therefore an understanding mind to govern your people, able to discern between good and evil; for who can govern this your great people?"

• • •

When my son David's reign was over, his son Solomon, all of 20 years old, inherited the throne. His beginnings, like his father's, were humble and seeking of my counsel. He knew that when someone is in charge of a people, they should be humbled by the task and responsibility of caring for the people's well-being. It saddens me deeply that my son Solomon could not retain that wisdom. Today I ask you to pray for leaders in your midst, that they might ground themselves in humility for your sake, for my sake, and for the sake of those entrusted to their care. Seek also that same humility for those entrusted to your care, for I have entrusted you with responsibility for many, now and in the future.

April 4

Hebrews 4:15

• • •

For we do not have a high priest who is unable to sympathize with our weaknesses, but we have one who in every respect has been tested as we are, yet without sin.

• • •

I know that sometimes it is daunting to follow my Son, who is known to be patient and loving and righteous and wise. And yet he knows your journey, and he knows the challenges that life poses. He knows struggle and hunger and rejection and mourning. He knows temptation. And instead of a priest looking down on you with judgment, you have a brother who walks with you, who wants you to be fed and joy-filled and free. Today I invite you to reflect on Jesus as your sibling, one who knows what you're going through and wants to offer support on your journey, and one who invites you to share with him any trouble you bear.

April 5

2 Kings 2:11–12

• • •

As they continued walking and talking, a chariot of fire and horses of fire separated the two of them, and Elijah ascended in a whirlwind into heaven. Elisha kept watching and crying out, "Father, father! The chariots of Israel and its horsemen!" But when he could no longer see him, he grasped his own clothes and tore them in two pieces.

• • •

Elijah was a miracle-making prophet who took Elisha under his wing when I told him Elisha would follow in his footsteps. They weren't blood relatives, and Elisha had lots of warning that Elijah would be leaving. And yet when it happened, Elisha was devastated. When you connect with others of my followers, my hope is that you create family, that you support and love each other. But this means the loss you experience will be real. I will be there to love you through it, and to help you grieve in all the ways you need to. Because I love and value you as much as I did your spiritual ancestors Elijah and Elisha, who stood up to kings and raised the dead and provided miracles to care for widows and orphans. Today I invite you to let me in to provide love and compassion amidst any grief you face.

April 6

James 1:19-21

• • •

You must understand this, my beloved: let everyone be quick to listen, slow to speak, slow to anger; for your anger does not produce God's righteousness. Therefore rid yourselves of all sordidness and rank growth of wickedness, and welcome with meekness the implanted word that has the power to save your souls.

• • •

You have a right to all of your emotions (as long as they don't hurt others), but when my beloved son wrote this letter he was reminding you that in community it can be easy to assume things and become angry without getting the full context. Being quick to listen is an important guideline in the community of saints, so that you can focus your anger where it matters: at injustice and poverty and mistreatment of my children. This is a hard practice, I know. But today I want you to consider what it would be like to invite several people to join you in this practice of being quick to listen, slow to speak, and slow to anger. Imagine what your community could feel like if you began to practice this spiritual discipline together, and what a different place it might feel like to others in need of a listening ear and less judgment.

April 7

1 Chronicles 15:16

• • •

David also commanded the chiefs of the Levites to appoint their kindred as the singers to play on musical instruments, on harps and lyres and cymbals, to raise loud sounds of joy.

• • •

My children sing a song, "Little David play on your harp, hallelu, hallelu!" and it brings me great joy. My son David, from childhood through kinghood, knew that he worshiped a God who loves to see children experiencing joy. Worship should not be a dreary task to get through; it should help you feel a little taste of the joy I have in store for you. Singers, harps, cymbals, and loud sounds help you connect to your playful, childlike side. So today I invite you to do something that helps you connect to the joy deep inside you, and know that I made you for joy. You might even want to sing to me; I do not need a beautiful noise, just a joyful one, to make my heart sing with yours.

April 8

1 Peter 2:4-6

• • •

Come to him, a living stone, though rejected by mortals yet chosen and precious in God's sight, and like living stones, let yourselves be built into a spiritual house, to be a holy priesthood, to offer spiritual sacrifices acceptable to God through Jesus Christ. For it stands in scripture:
"See, I am laying in Zion a stone,
a cornerstone chosen and precious;
and whoever believes in him will not be put to shame."

• • •

It is so easy to feel inadequate for the task to which I've called you. And it's so easy to see the imperfections of the others with whom I've called you into community. Today's scripture is a reminder to you: I love you in your imperfections. I love you in the ways that you don't fit in or feel like you are misunderstood. I am building a world with you and your imperfect, misunderstood siblings. Today I invite you to see if you can tap into a little bit of my grace toward those in your community who frustrate you. And I invite you to remember that the parts of you the world has rejected are the parts of you that I love the most.

April 9

2 Chronicles 13:18

• • •

Thus the Israelites were subdued at that time, and the people of Judah prevailed, because they relied on the LORD, the God of their ancestors.

• • •

A time in your spiritual history that broke my heart was when my children warred with each other. Every time my children fight and kill and die in my name is painful. Your spiritual ancestors split in those days, the Israelites and the Judeans. Many even forgot their relationship with me in the midst of their battles. Today I invite you to consider what kind of world would be possible if you relied on me, the God of your ancestors. Where might you prevail? Where might I show up in your work and in your life and in your heart if you relied on me as the people of Judah did so long ago?

April 10

2 Peter 1:5–8

• • •

For this very reason, you must make every effort to support your faith with goodness, and goodness with knowledge, and knowledge with self-control, and self-control with endurance, and endurance with godliness, and godliness with mutual affection, and mutual affection with love. For if these things are yours and are increasing among you, they keep you from being ineffective and unfruitful in the knowledge of our Lord Jesus Christ.

• • •

Today I want you to write out a chart:

faith ⟵— goodness ⟵— knowledge ⟵—
self-control ⟵— endurance ⟵— godliness ⟵—
mutual affection ⟵— love

Each is undergirded by the one before it. And note that my servant wrote "increasing among you," not just within you. This is a guide for your community. I want you to write what it would look like for love to manifest in your community right now, and how that would lead to mutual affection, to godliness, to endurance, to self-control, to knowledge, to goodness, and ultimately to faith. And then I want you to write down your role in helping those things happen. You are a critical part of building my realm here on earth. May you be strengthened for that work today.

April 11

Ezra 3:11b-13

• • •

And all the people responded with a great shout when they praised the Lord, because the foundation of the house of the Lord was laid. But many of the priests and Levites and heads of families, old people who had seen the first house on its foundations, wept with a loud voice when they saw this house, though many shouted aloud for joy, so that the people could not distinguish the sound of the joyful shout from the sound of the people's weeping, for the people shouted so loudly that the sound was heard far away.

• • •

Change can be a gift. Change can be painful. And sometimes the same change can be a gift to some and painful to others. There are few spaces where feelings of joy and feelings of loss can be honored side by side like they were when your spiritual ancestors in Israel got to rebuild their temple to me after returning from exile in Babylon. Where in the world today do you witness both mourning and joy side by side? When do you feel both things side by side even within yourself? How can that combination honor me? Today I invite you to reflect on how to create space for both joy and mourning for yourself and those around you, that you might be more whole, and more connected to both your humanity and your sacredness, so we might grow closer.

April 12

1 John 2:4-6

• • •

Whoever says, "I have come to know him," but does not obey his commandments, is a liar, and in such a person the truth does not exist; but whoever obeys his word, truly in this person the love of God has reached perfection. By this we may be sure that we are in him: whoever says, "I abide in him," ought to walk just as he walked.

• • •

One of my faithful servants, Henry Lyte, was orphaned and taken in by a pastor who helped him become a faithful follower of mine who served the poor and sick until he wore himself out. In his final sermon 10 weeks before passing away from tuberculosis, he wrote the hymn "Abide with Me," inviting me into his presence in those final days. I abide with all my children. Abiding with me, however, calls for a life like that of my beloved son Henry, serving in love, caring for those around you because you know that they carry my divine spark within them. Today reflect on the fact that I will always abide with you and ask yourself how you might abide with me today.

April 13

Nehemiah 2:17b–20a

• • •

"Come, let us rebuild the wall of Jerusalem, so that we may no longer suffer disgrace." I told them that the hand of my God had been gracious upon me, and also the words that the king had spoken to me. Then they said, "Let us start building!" So they committed themselves to the common good. But when Sanballat the Horonite and Tobiah the Ammonite official, and Geshem the Arab heard of it, they mocked and ridiculed us, saying, "What is this that you are doing? Are you rebelling against the king?" Then I replied to them, "The God of heaven is the one who will give us success, and we his servants are going to start building; but you have no share or claim or historic right in Jerusalem."

• • •

People in your era often say, "history is written by the victors." Nehemiah heard me calling on him to bring Jerusalem back to its former glory. And yet my son Sanballat, a Samaritan, had been living with his community there faithfully worshiping me when the Israelites returned from exile. Part of me aches for the way my children could not find common ground or create space for each other. Today I invite you to think about the conflicts you face with others even as you seek to follow me. Pray for wisdom about how to both follow my will and love your neighbor.

April 14

2 John 1:5

• • •

But now, dear lady, I ask you, not as though I were writing you a new commandment, but one we have had from the beginning, let us love one another.

• • •

Simple and easy are not the same thing. As simple as the commandment "love one another" seems, it is also the hardest thing I ask of you. I know you have been hurt. I know that love can make you feel vulnerable. I know my children are complicated. And I call you to this ancient commandment because it actually helps you be the powerful person I know you to be. When you love others, you overcome fear. When you love others, you bring my Son's presence into a world that needs Him. When you love others, our connection grows stronger. Today I invite you to extend loving compassion to the people around you, and to recognize my power flowing through you whenever you do it. You are my beloved child. Today be loved and be love.

April 15

Esther 2:19–20

• • •

When the virgins were being gathered together, Mordecai was sitting at the king's gate. Now Esther had not revealed her kindred or her people, as Mordecai had charged her; for Esther obeyed Mordecai just as when she was brought up by him.

• • •

My beloved daughter Esther was hiding in plain sight. In a nation that distrusted Jewish people, her uncle told her not to advertise her faith and culture, because he wanted her to stay safe. How often my children end up having to hide parts of who they are in order to stay safe in a world ruled by fear, hatred, and ignorance. I long for a better world for you, for your siblings, for your children, and their children. Today I invite you to pray for an end to hatred, fear, and ignorance, and I invite you to turn to me, that you might be an instrument for love, courage, and compassionate wisdom.

April 16

John 2:15–16

• • •

Making a whip of cords, he drove all of them out of the temple, both the sheep and the cattle. He also poured out the coins of the money changers and overturned their tables. He told those who were selling the doves, "Take these things out of here! Stop making my Father's house a marketplace!"

• • •

Many say that my Son's rage was directed at people making my temple less holy. That is true, but what enraged him most was how poor people, traveling from far away, were gouged. They wanted to honor me, and they could not bring sacrifices from so far away. The people selling doves in the marketplace, knowing the birds were all that the poorest worshipers could afford, marked up the prices grievously. My Son's outrage at the thieves in the temple reflected my own outrage at the mistreatment of my poorest followers. Today I invite you to reflect on how to cultivate your own outrage at the way my treasured children are treated and how to stand up against their mistreatment, so that you and I may grow closer and closer day by day.

April 17

Job 10:2-3

• • •

I will say to God, Do not condemn me;
    let me know why you contend against me.
Does it seem good to you to oppress,
    to despise the work of your hands
    and favor the schemes of the wicked?

• • •

My faithful child Job asked a question that so many of my children have asked: why do the good suffer and the evil prevail? So often my children cry out to me, "Where are you in the face of this injustice?" And over and over I say, "I am there. I am there because I have sent you, and I made you in my image." Job had gone through life being a good and decent person in his own spaces. He had not noticed how those around him suffered despite being good. This was a critical part of his journey to grow closer to me. Today I invite you to ask yourself where you witness the schemes of the wicked prevailing, and which other people also made in my image you can join with to resist their schemes.

April 18

Jude 1:21

• • •

...keep yourselves in the love of God; look forward to the mercy of our Lord Jesus Christ that leads to eternal life.

• • •

In your life there are so many ways to fall short. One of my children once said that the Christian life is a life of trying to do the least harm, because simply buying cereal impacts farmers and field workers and truckers and factory workers and grocery clerks. Your life is already pointed towards me, yet you have fallen short and you will fall short again. In those moments, I want you never to forget my overwhelming, ever present grace and mercy, my seven-times-seventy commitment to forgiving you as you strive always to do right by all of my children and by me. I see you. I love you. I forgive you, today and always. And I am at your back as you seek to do right, even when you falter or fail. Pay attention today; see if you can feel me there, supporting you at every turn.

April 19

Psalms 25:14–15

• • •

The friendship of the LORD is for those who fear him,
and he makes his covenant known to them.
My eyes are ever toward the LORD,
for he will pluck my feet out of the net.

• • •

Whenever you feel trapped, remember that I am there with you to free you. I know the path I have set for you is not an easy one. I know that there are people in your life seeking to pull you off that path. Today I simply want you to feel my presence in that place where you feel trapped. I want you to picture me untangling you. I want you to experience those feet being able to escape the net and rejoin the path that we get to walk together. And I want you to know that every time your feet get caught in a net, I will show up to untangle you again.

April 20

Revelation 3:1b–3

• • •

"I know your works; you have a name for being alive, but you are dead. Wake up, and strengthen what remains and is on the point of death, for I have not found your works perfect in the sight of my God. Remember then what you received and heard; obey it, and repent."

• • •

So many faith communities rest on their reputation or even simply their stories about themselves. What was true 2,000 years ago when John of Patmos received his revelation remains true today: I honor and am honored only by a church that is constantly striving to better do my will in the world. I have little patience with a community that gathers on Sunday but does nothing to serve my children the rest of the week. Today I invite you to pray for my passion and love and Spirit of justice to flood those communities, that they might live. I invite you to pray for your role in helping your own faith community to live as I would have it live, standing up against injustice and nurturing the well-being and gifts of my children who are ignored by the rest of society.

April 21

Proverbs 8:1-6

• • •

Does not wisdom call,
    and does not understanding raise her voice?
On the heights, beside the way,
    at the crossroads she takes her stand;
beside the gates in front of the town,
    at the entrance of the portals she cries out:
"To you, O people, I call,
    and my cry is to all that live.
O simple ones, learn prudence;
    acquire intelligence, you who lack it.
Hear, for I will speak noble things,
    and from my lips will come what is right."

• • •

You can hear my voice on Main Street, at the busiest intersection on Wall Street, in front of the grocery store and the town hall...and by the city gates at the time my child wrote this part of Proverbs. Wisdom's instructions are still true today. When you hear words of dignity and justice and wisdom, even when car horns and cash registers and the clanging of closing bells try to drown those words out: that's me. Today I invite you to listen for wisdom in the midst of folly and greed and fear. And when you hear it, I invite you to repeat it to others you value.

April 22

Matthew 3:16–17

• • •

And when Jesus had been baptized, just as he came up from the water, suddenly the heavens were opened to him and he saw the Spirit of God descending like a dove and alighting on him. And a voice from heaven said, "This is my Son, the Beloved, with whom I am well pleased."

• • •

Your generation and many before you emphasized how Jesus was uniquely my child. That is true. But it is also true that YOU are uniquely my child. When I see you, I see my spirit alighting on you. You are my child, my beloved, with whom I am well pleased. Today I invite you to look in the mirror and tell yourself exactly that: "I am God's beloved child with whom God is well pleased." And I want you to find someone else who needs to hear this, and tell them the same thing.

April 23

Ecclesiastes 3:1-4

• • •

For everything there is a season, and a time for every matter under heaven:

a time to be born, and a time to die;
a time to plant, and a time to pluck up what is planted;
a time to kill, and a time to heal;
a time to break down, and a time to build up;
a time to weep, and a time to laugh;
a time to mourn, and a time to dance.

• • •

I know you have faced seasons glorious and hard and in-between. If you are facing a hard season right now, I invite you to pray for the endurance to survive it, and the gifts and community and wisdom to transform it. If you are living through a glorious season, I invite you to pray for how to really appreciate it, how to make the most of its gifts, and how to let that glory ripple out so others benefit from it as well. My deepest wish is that you would find connections with me and my people that would soften the blow of the hard seasons and allow us to rejoice together in the good ones.

April 24

Mark 4:21-22

• • •

He said to them, "Is a lamp brought in to be put under the bushel basket, or under the bed, and not on the lampstand? For there is nothing hidden, except to be disclosed; nor is anything secret, except to come to light."

• • •

When my Son said these words, he was honoring the fact that my light, the light of the Holy Spirit, dwells in YOU. The world may try to hide your light or tell you that you do not radiate with my light. But hiding things and keeping secrets can be a tool of evil. Efforts to diminish your radiance are also a tool of evil. Today I invite you to notice where my light shines in you. And if you are feeling brave and particularly faithful, notice where it shines in the people who frustrate you. Who has told them their light is dim, so that they seek to diminish yours? My hope is that all my children will recognize their own divine light so they can also recognize each other's.

April 25

Song of Solomon 1:5

• • •

I am black and beautiful,
   O daughters of Jerusalem,
like the tents of Kedar,
   like the curtains of Solomon.

• • •

I find so much joy in the diverse and glorious perfection of my creation, made in my image, all genders and shapes and shades and cultures. Some of my children, seeking power, perpetuate the lie that light skin is more beautiful than dark. I am so glad that my beloved child who wrote Song of Songs knew to celebrate the beauty of Blackness. I am so glad this truth has stood for millennia in the face of power-seeking people's lies. I created you in my image. And my image is vast. Today offer up a prayer of gratitude for the diverse gifts and beauty in you and the rest of my children who together represent my vastness.

April 26

Luke 6:20b-21

• • •

"Blessed are you who are poor,
    for yours is the kingdom of God.
"Blessed are you who are hungry now,
    for you will be filled.
"Blessed are you who weep now,
    for you will laugh."

• • •

You may have noticed that throughout the Bible, I choose second sons instead of first sons. I choose sex workers. I choose old people whom society discounts. I choose youth. I choose poor people. Part of your task as my child, carrying my divine light in you, is to help create a world where I do not have to choose people on the margins over and over because the world you create has no margins. I know you cannot by yourself create a world where all my children are equally valued. Today pray to connect with others who will work with you to create a world right here where those who weep will laugh and those who are hungry will be filled. Know that I love you and want that same world for you.

April 27

Isaiah 42:13–14

• • •

The LORD goes forth like a soldier,
    like a warrior he stirs up his fury;
he cries out, he shouts aloud,
    he shows himself mighty against his foes.
For a long time I have held my peace,
    I have kept still and restrained myself;
now I will cry out like a woman in labor,
    I will gasp and pant.

• • •

My child wrote this trusting in your capacity to grasp metaphors and with a need for you to understand the urgency of moments when my children are suffering. I abhor cruelty; I have a mighty fury about injustice. It is a visceral pain to me like the pain of childbirth. I need you to join me as a peaceful warrior against the mistreatment of my children—those who go hungry, those trapped in lands saturated with war, those facing economic and sexual exploitation. Today I ask you to strap on the armor of spiritual warfare: the sword of truth, the shield of compassion, the breastplate of peace. In an era that requires politeness but tolerates violence, this is a deeply countercultural calling. This moment is as urgent as any moment on the battlefield. Will you join me there?

April 28

John 4:27

• • •

Just then his disciples came. They were astonished that he was speaking with a woman, but no one said, "What do you want?" or, "Why are you speaking with her?"

• • •

Because so many of my Son's followers focus on His divinity, they sometimes miss out on His tendency to be a troublemaker. Then again most of them don't notice that about me either. Jesus was hanging out with a woman who was treated badly by the other townspeople, so badly that she discouraged Jesus from talking with her. I wish Jesus' disciples *had* asked him that question, so he could remind them that the divine spark in her was just as powerful as it was in them. His disciples worried that His association with her would make Him (and them) look bad. Jesus knew that people can only be judged by who they choose to be, not by how society views the people with whom they associate. I hope the divine spark in you causes you today to ignore society's norms and draws you to people who need a reminder of the divine spark within them when the world seeks to quash it out.

April 29

Jeremiah 17:5-6a, 7-8a

• • •

Thus says the LORD:
Cursed are those who trust in mere mortals
    and make mere flesh their strength,
      whose hearts turn away from the LORD.
They shall be like a shrub in the desert,
    and shall not see when relief comes.
Blessed are those who trust in the LORD,
    whose trust is the LORD.
They shall be like a tree planted by water,
    sending out its roots by the stream.

• • •

I know you have had moments when you have felt let down by people in your life. While the best of my children seek to grow closer to the divine perfection born into them, humans fall short. Love the people around you, build community with them, forgive them when they let you down. But know that even when people break your heart, I will be there to hold you and comfort you. What would it look like for you to place less trust in human structures and institutions and to trust me more fully? How can you invest more deeply in us, so that you might be more grounded as you work to grow closer to divine perfection?

April 30

Acts 5:38-39

• • •

So in the present case, I tell you, keep away from these men and let them alone; because if this plan or this undertaking is of human origin, it will fail; but if it is of God, you will not be able to overthrow them—in that case you may even be found fighting against God!

• • •

My beloved son Gamaliel, a Pharisee (Jewish legal scholar), remains beloved by both my Jewish and Christian children for his great wisdom, restraint, and faithfulness. Some people (including at the time Saul, who became my faithful son Paul) wanted to kill my Son's disciples for what felt like blasphemy. Gamaliel said that if those disciples were setting out to do something nefarious, it would unravel, and if it was my will, they should let it thrive and not get in the way of God. So often my children are consumed by petty concerns over who gets credit or what people's motives are. Today I invite you to practice focusing on doing my will in the world rather than being consumed with others' actions. Trust that your acts of good will align with the good of others and will bring to light the acts that are out of alignment with my will.

May

May 1

Lamentations 1:18

• • •

The LORD is in the right,
for I have rebelled against his word;
but hear, all you peoples,
and behold my suffering;
my young women and young men
have gone into captivity.

• • •

I call on you to be faithful, but if you are really of me, then how can your heart not break when so many of my children are harmed by sins that are not theirs? As many as 30 million people are in captivity, in human bondage or enslavement, in the world today. They suffer because economic conditions or violence at home pushed them there, or because farms in neighboring countries profit more with child labor, or for many other reasons related to the sins of greed and violence. Today I ask you to hold my pain with me for my beloved children in captivity today. I ask you to explore how to participate in their liberation.

May 2

Romans 5:3–5

• • •

And not only that, but we also boast in our sufferings, knowing that suffering produces endurance, and endurance produces character, and character produces hope, and hope does not disappoint us, because God's love has been poured into our hearts through the Holy Spirit that has been given to us.

• • •

I want to be clear as crystal: I do not want you to suffer. I did not want the author of this text, Paul, to suffer. I want to cocreate with you a world where suffering is no longer. This passage has been abused to tell people to tolerate abuse, and that was neither Paul's intent nor mine. What is true is this: when people seek to create a world that values everyone, the people who profit from the world as it is will seek to punish the changemakers. And so Paul offered a word of comfort to the people being punished for creating a more loving and inclusive and compassionate world. If you suffer for your faithfulness to the work of building a compassionate world, know that I will never abandon you, that I am proud of you, that my Spirit accompanies you through all of your troubles. Today pray for an end to suffering and comfort for those suffering.

May 3

Ezekiel 18:1-3

• • •

The word of the LORD came to me: What do you mean by repeating this proverb concerning the land of Israel, "The parents have eaten sour grapes, and the children's teeth are set on edge"? As I live, says the Lord GOD, this proverb shall no more be used by you in Israel.

• • •

Another way of saying this is that the sins of the father are visited on the children. Too often this is heartbreakingly true: when a parent makes a bad decision, the child suffers the consequences, from womb to grave. And yet to embrace this as an inevitability, to prop up a caste system where people are trapped in their clan or the status of their birth or shunned for who their parents are, offended me 2,500 years ago when Ezekiel spoke it, and it offends me today. So I invite you to dream with me a world where my children do not blame or isolate or castigate someone for their parents' mistakes or for accidents of birth, but you allow them to navigate the world as their own, individual selves.

May 4

1 Corinthians 5:6–7a

• • •

Your boasting is not a good thing. Do you not know that a little yeast leavens the whole batch of dough? Clean out the old yeast so that you may be a new batch, as you really are unleavened.

• • •

When my son Paul wrote this, he knew that a community cannot thrive when a few people's negative behavior holds the rest of the community back. What will save and heal your generation is the creation of a community where people are measured by their acts of compassion and care for each other. That is the new yeast that will help you all rise as a community. Today pray for guidance about how your community may receive some new yeast of humility and compassion and clean out the old yeast of boasting and "me first," so that you may thrive.

May 5

Daniel 6:26b-27

• • •

"For he is the living God,
    enduring forever.
His kingdom shall never be destroyed,
    and his dominion has no end.
He delivers and rescues,
    he works signs and wonders in heaven and on earth;
for he has saved Daniel
    from the power of the lions."

• • •

These words were spoken by King Darius because he saw Daniel's faith. Even though Darius and his kingdom worshiped other gods, Daniel and other Jewish people risked their lives to remain faithful to me. Some scholars point to how this book is historically inaccurate, but what I ask you to reflect on is this: it was a book of comfort and encouragement written to a people trying to survive in a world that kept trying to kill them for their faith. Who in your life needs a word of comfort and encouragement? Who can you bolster today when they seek to honor me and feel worn down? May you be a balm to them, as the book of Daniel has been to my people for generations.

May 6

2 Corinthians 5:1

• • •

For we know that if the earthly tent we live in is destroyed, we have a building from God, a house not made with hands, eternal in the heavens.

• • •

For millennia, people have celebrated that the sacred texts can speak on multiple levels. This verse reminds you that no matter what you endure on earth, you have comfort ahead. It offers encouragement that when you leave this world, there is another world waiting for you. And yet you as a faithful child know that it is not my will that my children be unsheltered. In the hereafter, those who suffered unnecessarily in this world will know comfort and abundance for eternity. But this passage does not mean it is okay for people to suffer homelessness. Today take comfort in knowing that whatever challenges this world throws at you, I will show up for you over and over, and I will be there to embrace you in the world yet to come. And I invite you to pray that my children know comfort in this world as well.

May 7

Hosea 6:3

• • •

Let us know, let us press on to know the LORD;
    his appearing is as sure as the dawn;
he will come to us like the showers,
    like the spring rains that water the earth.

• • •

In the land where Hosea lived, rains could be erratic and unreliable—too little and the crops would die, too much and the plains would flood. Here is what you need to know about my love: it is constant and reliable. And even if it feels like too much love, if you've been told that you don't deserve to be showered with love, it will always be enough to make you flourish. This passage was written in the plural because I am there for your whole community as much as I am there for you, amidst the droughts and floods, completely reliable, completely invested in you and your people.

May 8

Galatians 2:9–10

• • •

...and when James and Cephas and John, who were acknowledged pillars, recognized the grace that had been given to me, they gave to Barnabas and me the right hand of fellowship, agreeing that we should go to the Gentiles and they to the circumcised. They asked only one thing, that we remember the poor, which was actually what I was eager to do.

• • •

My imperfect but deeply faithful son Paul speaks to a beautiful moment in your history: when the Jesus-following Jews agreed to extend to non-Jewish people an invitation into relationship with me. Every time the invitation into love is spread wider among my children, it makes my heart glad. There is a famous saying among some Christians: In essentials, unity; in non-essentials, liberty; in all things, charity. It also makes my heart glad that the essential of all these early Jesus followers was to care for the poor, whom Jesus loves and whom I love. Today I invite you to imagine how your community can center on that essential ever more deeply and extend the invitation into my love ever more widely, for the sake of your community's thriving.

May 9

Joel 2:1–2

• • •

Blow the trumpet in Zion;
    sound the alarm on my holy mountain!
Let all the inhabitants of the land tremble,
    for the day of the LORD is coming, it is near—
a day of darkness and gloom,
    a day of clouds and thick darkness!
Like blackness spread upon the mountains
    a great and powerful army comes;
their like has never been from of old,
    nor will be again after them
    in ages to come.

• • •

In the days of my beloved son Joel, locusts ravaged the land. The people believed it was my punishment for their wrongdoing. The sad truth is that my children, particularly the kings and rulers I warned you about, are always engaging in activity that raises my ire. And the land itself fights back. Humanity is right to be afraid of the consequences of its actions; it just directs that fear at me instead of the land that humanity tortures instead of stewarding. Today I ask you to pay attention to how the land is fighting back against its gross mistreatment and pray for guidance in how to help your people once again become stewards of the land instead of torturers.

May 10

Ephesians 3:13

• • •

I pray therefore that you may not lose heart over my sufferings for you; they are your glory.

• • •

Some of my children are incarcerated because of their actions. Some are placed in prison and jail because the situation they were born into gave them almost no chance to survive without breaking the law. Some are falsely incarcerated by a system that does not provide equal justice to all. Some end up in prison because the state is terrified of their beliefs. It can be terrifying to a community to lose a leader because of their beliefs, and the author of Ephesians extended comfort and encouragement to a people afraid for their future. Everyone in prison is a beloved child of mine, no matter what brought them there, and too often the injustices of this world played a role in their incarceration. Pray today for all of your siblings in prison, for compassion or transformation or liberation or justice.

May 11

Amos 5:11–12

• • •

Therefore, because you trample on the poor
    and take from them levies of grain,
you have built houses of hewn stone,
    but you shall not live in them;
you have planted pleasant vineyards,
    but you shall not drink their wine.
For I know how many are your transgressions,
    and how great are your sins—
you who afflict the righteous, who take a bribe,
    and push aside the needy in the gate.

• • •

Your sacred texts speak more than 2,000 times about poverty, about my call for compassion and abundance and support of the poor. Today I invite you to pray that those in power would be either transformed or dethroned for the sake of ending corruption, and that those who would replace them focus instead on building up systems and structures that take care of those in need.

May 12

Philippians 2:3–4

• • •

Do nothing from selfish ambition or conceit, but in humility regard others as better than yourselves. Let each of you look not to your own interests, but to the interests of others.

• • •

This is the world I want for you: where your siblings place your needs first and you do the same for them, and by placing others before yourselves, your needs are met. Today I invite you to share this vision with someone you value, and instead of focusing on how people are too greedy for it to work, begin to dream of how you could build that community starting with the two of you and letting the power of that vision ripple outward.

May 13

Obadiah 1:6–7

• • •

How Esau has been pillaged,
  his treasures searched out!
All your allies have deceived you,
  they have driven you to the border;
your confederates have prevailed against you;
  those who ate your bread have set a trap for you—
  there is no understanding of it.

• • •

My children in Edom lived on the margins of Judah and resented their lowly status. They helped Babylon pillage Jerusalem, and my son Obadiah reminded them that when they chose a people not their own over their family, their foreign allies would not care for them. I wish that no such suffering would befall you. When you face conflict with your siblings in the faith, have the conflict in the open. If you cannot reconcile, then part for the sake of each other's thriving and do not plot secretly with people who have neither your nor your siblings' well-being at heart. Today I invite you to pray for the discipline of transparency and spiritual maturity to protect you from the harm that comes to the schemer as well as to the schemed against.

May 14

Colossians 2:6-7

• • •

As you therefore have received Christ Jesus the Lord, continue to live your lives in him, rooted and built up in him and established in the faith, just as you were taught, abounding in thanksgiving.

• • •

The practice of gratitude can get you through some incredibly hard times. As you root yourself in my Son, you'll find those roots growing stronger and stronger as you pause to reflect on where there is beauty, generosity, compassion, and love in your life and offering up a word of thanks to me. As I have said before, I do not seek gratitude because I am a vain God. I seek it because it is medicine to the souls of my children. Today I invite you to offer thanks for at least five things in your life, and I ask you to see how many days you can maintain that practice and observe what happens to your heart the longer you do it.

May 15

Jonah 2:1–2

• • •

Then Jonah prayed to the Lᴏʀᴅ his God from the belly of the fish, saying,
> "I called to the Lᴏʀᴅ out of my distress,
>   and he answered me;
> out of the belly of Sheol I cried,
>   and you heard my voice."

• • •

There is nowhere you can wind up that I will not be able to hear your cry. Even if your suffering is of your own making, that will not stop me from showing up for you. Even if you are running away from me, like Jonah, I will be ready to embrace you when you turn to me again. If I can liberate Jonah from the belly of the big fish, I can liberate you from whatever is trapping you. Today I invite you to offer me your pain and your struggles, your resentments and your shame; I want to carry them for you. You do not need to navigate this world alone.

May 16

1 Thessalonians 4:10–12

• • •

...and indeed you do love all the brothers and sisters throughout Macedonia. But we urge you, beloved, to do so more and more, to aspire to live quietly, to mind your own affairs, and to work with your hands, as we directed you, so that you may behave properly toward outsiders and be dependent on no one.

• • •

The world you live in is ugly in how it has replaced reciprocity (mutual exchange) with transactional relationships (paying for things and not being in relationship with the people who provide what you need). My child who wrote 1 Thessalonians did not want his community beholden to others who would exploit or harm them, so he invited them to create a community set a little apart, doing harm to no one, not antagonizing others but making sure they could care for each other without being beholden to those who would harm them. What would it look like for your community to do the same, to be self-sufficient, to take care of each other so that you do not have to rely on those who would exploit your reliance on them, but you could still extend compassion and hospitality to those who are not part of your community?

May 17

Micah 4:3-4

• • •

He shall judge between many peoples,
　　and shall arbitrate between strong nations far away;
they shall beat their swords into plowshares,
　　and their spears into pruning hooks;
nation shall not lift up sword against nation,
　　neither shall they learn war any more;
but they shall all sit under their own vines and under their
own fig trees,
　　and no one shall make them afraid;
　　for the mouth of the Lord of hosts has spoken.

• • •

What a world that will be. Today all I ask is that you spend time picturing a world without weapons, without global conflict, without even planning for conflict, where people are cared for, have time to rest, and live unafraid. Pray that you and I can work together to make it so.

May 18

2 Thessalonians 2:1-2

• • •

As to the coming of our Lord Jesus Christ and our being gathered together to him, we beg you, brothers and sisters, not to be quickly shaken in mind or alarmed, either by spirit or by word or by letter, as though from us, to the effect that the day of the Lord is already here.

• • •

All I have ever asked is that you focus on living well with each other and let me arrive in my time, which is not yours. Today I invite you to pray for patience in the places where you want instant change, and for courage to live as if my realm is already here on earth, that in so doing, you help further it.

May 19

Nahum 1:15

• • •

Look! On the mountains the feet of one
    who brings good tidings,
    who proclaims peace!

• • •

There is no greater news than that of peace—true peace, not simply a lack of conflict propped up by the suffering of or injustice toward some for the benefit of others. Today I invite you to pray that your life might be such that one day the people will proclaim about you with the same enthusiasm as the people in Nahum's time, "Look! On the mountains the feet of one who brings good tidings, who proclaims peace!"

May 20

1 Timothy 4:4-5

• • •

For everything created by God is good, and nothing is to be rejected, provided it is received with thanksgiving; for it is sanctified by God's word and by prayer.

• • •

Today I invite you to notice everything created by me and treat it as sacred. Notice what you honor, and what does not get designated as sacred. How might that change what you eat, what you watch and listen to, and how you engage all of my children you interact with, the land on which you walk, and all of my creatures you engage today?

May 21

Habakkuk 1:13

• • •

Your eyes are too pure to behold evil,
and you cannot look on wrongdoing;
why do you look on the treacherous,
and are silent when the wicked swallow
those more righteous than they?

• • •

My beloved son Habakkuk asked me this question, and I could hear his sense of both betrayal and confusion, and it broke my heart. You may have heard the joke where I respond to him, "I was going to ask you the same question." You and I are in this together. Just like Habakkuk and I were coconspirators in ending corruption and injustice, you and I are coconspirators. You're my justice warrior there on earth...a superhero of sorts. Today I invite you to embrace your anger at injustice, to ask me the hard questions like Habakkuk did, and to invite me to partner with you in our work together to create a world where the righteous triumph over the wicked.

May 22

2 Timothy 2:8-9

• • •

Remember Jesus Christ, raised from the dead, a descendant of David—that is my gospel, for which I suffer hardship, even to the point of being chained like a criminal. But the word of God is not chained.

• • •

I know that you cannot take freedom for granted when there are people who seek to rule, exploit those at the bottom of the ladder and silence those who speak out for compassion, truth, and justice. And yet throughout history, over and over, tyrants have fallen and justice has replaced them. It is a constant struggle, but my word is not chained. Today I invite you to pray that the good news of life after death, the good news of freedom for the captives, the good news of love and liberation may ever be of service to you in your calling to serve me.

May 23

Zephaniah 1:12–13

• • •

At that time I will search Jerusalem with lamps,
　　and I will punish the people
who rest complacently on their dregs,
　　those who say in their hearts,
"The Lord will not do good,
　　nor will he do harm."
Their wealth shall be plundered,
　　and their houses laid waste.
Though they build houses,
　　they shall not inhabit them;
though they plant vineyards,
　　they shall not drink wine from them.

• • •

The reason that greed and fear are the shadow sides of each other is that those who are greedy have reason to fear. Those who have taken resources for which others have labored can never rest easy, knowing that they have harmed others for their own comfort. They may not realize that they should fear me, but they have built their houses on rocky terrain and can never be free of the fear that their actions will come back to haunt them. Today I invite you to pray that those who have received their resources in exploitive ways may see the error of those ways, repent, and do right by those who suffered before it is too late.

May 24

Titus 1:15–16a

• • •

To the pure all things are pure, but to the corrupt and unbelieving nothing is pure. Their very minds and consciences are corrupted. They profess to know God, but they deny him by their actions.

• • •

Today I offer you one task: reflect on what people know about you by your actions and on whether those actions speak to your faith in me. Invite me into a conversation about how to support the ways in which your life honors me, and about how to help you develop new patterns in the areas where you do not yet honor me with how you go through the world. We are on this journey together, my beloved child.

May 25

Haggai 2:4-5

• • •

Yet now take courage, O Zerubbabel, says the LORD; take courage, O Joshua, son of Jehozadak, the high priest; take courage, all you people of the land, says the LORD; work, for I am with you, says the LORD of hosts, according to the promise that I made you when you came out of Egypt. My spirit abides among you; do not fear.

• • •

When my children got to return to the land of their ancestors after exile to Babylon, my beloved son Haggai encouraged them to invest themselves in building once again a temple in which they could gather to worship. Through him I reminded them not to fear, although they had experienced much fear and trauma over the course of two generations. You have likewise had reason to be afraid at times throughout your life. And I make the same promise to you: take courage and invite your whole community to take courage and let go of fear. I am with you. I have freed you all before. I will be with you as you build again.

May 26

Philemon 1:7

• • •

I have indeed received much joy and encouragement from your love, because the hearts of the saints have been refreshed through you, my brother.

• • •

Think of an instance where you felt bolstered during a hard time. Even if you didn't realize I was there, I absolutely was. Some people have that innate gift of encouraging individuals and communities, supporting them in my behalf. I dream of an army of encouragers, replicating the work of the Holy Spirit as *paraclete*—advocate and encourager. Today I invite you to do the work of the Holy Spirit and encourage someone who is struggling, so that they might know I am with them, just as I am with you.

May 27

Zechariah 9:9

• • •

Rejoice greatly, O daughter Zion!
  Shout aloud, O daughter Jerusalem!
Lo, your king comes to you;
  triumphant and victorious is he,
humble and riding on a donkey,
  on a colt, the foal of a donkey.

• • •

For millennia, people have mistaken arrogance and brutality for true power. My power looks so different that humanity keeps missing it, even when it is right in front of them. Dictators recognize and fear it, which is why some of the greatest leaders of change, grounded in their humility, are killed. Humility is so powerful in a leader because a humble leader is secure in their dignity and self-worth so that they do not need to dominate others. Today I invite you to let me in, to recognize the innate dignity and divinity I placed in you, so that you too can be one of my humble servant leaders the world needs so much in the face of arrogant brutality in halls of power around the globe.

May 28

Hebrews 5:13–14

• • •

...for everyone who lives on milk, being still an infant, is unskilled in the word of righteousness. But solid food is for the mature, for those whose faculties have been trained by practice to distinguish good from evil.

• • •

The fact that you are on this spiritual journey with me shows that you seek to consume solid spiritual food, to go deeper. That does not mean becoming cynical or world weary. It just means knowing my vision for you more deeply, understanding the complexity and multilayered meaning of scripture more fully, and supporting those who are new to this journey. I need you right now to help those who are new to the work of faith and justice. Today notice the ways I have equipped you for this moment. Consider writing down a list so you remember your power in the times you feel shaky. You are who I called into this work, because I treasure you so much.

May 29

Malachi 1:11

· · ·

For from the rising of the sun to its setting my name is great among the nations, and in every place incense is offered to my name, and a pure offering; for my name is great among the nations, says the LORD of hosts.

· · ·

One of my beloved children once said, "our problem in the church is that we take ourselves too seriously and we don't take God seriously enough." What does it mean to take me seriously, to really center me in your life and make my role in your life matter more than the chatter and gossip and plotting and pettiness that humanity generates in an effort to take itself more seriously than it should? Today I invite you to reflect on what it is I want for your life, for your community, and for this world, and to invite me into the center of your life so that you might know real freedom of heart and mind.

May 30

James 1:22–25

• • •

But be doers of the word, and not merely hearers who deceive themselves. For if any are hearers of the word and not doers, they are like those who look at themselves in a mirror; for they look at themselves and, on going away, immediately forget what they were like. But those who look into the perfect law, the law of liberty, and persevere, being not hearers who forget but doers who act—they will be blessed in their doing.

• • •

Every teacher knows that action is the best reinforcer of knowledge. There are still seven months in this year. You will know who you are by what you do. Today I invite you to reflect on who you want to be this year and how your actions are leading you toward that...and toward me, who wants your thriving and the thriving of your community.

May 31

Psalms 33:20-21

• • •

Our soul waits for the LORD;
    he is our help and shield.
Our heart is glad in him,
    because we trust in his holy name.

• • •

Trust can come hard for my beloved children, because so many human beings have made it hard to trust. And because so often I am described as a father or a judge or a shepherd, the imperfect analogies used to describe me make me out to be a human. I am so much more than you can imagine, and I will always be worthy of your trust. The simple act of trust, of vulnerability, can be healing. Today I invite you to imagine what it would be like to be able to trust me, to be vulnerable to me, knowing that I will always be there for you as a shield and a help.

June

Liberating Love
JUN

365 LOVE NOTES
FROM GOD

June 1

Genesis 21:17–19

• • •

And God heard the voice of the boy; and the angel of God called to Hagar from heaven, and said to her, "What troubles you, Hagar? Do not be afraid; for God has heard the voice of the boy where he is. Come, lift up the boy and hold him fast with your hand, for I will make a great nation of him." Then God opened her eyes, and she saw a well of water. She went, and filled the skin with water, and gave the boy a drink.

• • •

Sometimes there are stories within stories. People often talk about the faithfulness of my beloved children Abraham and Sarah. They do not always celebrate my courageous and beautiful daughter Hagar. Hagar was enslaved, and her body was used to produce a child that she did not ask for, out of an act that had nothing to do with love. My daughter Hagar deserved better, as do all of my children forced into labor or sex trafficking or surrogacy. Today I ask you to offer up a prayer of celebration for Hagar's liberation and a prayer that your community might find ways to partner in bringing about people's liberation in your midst and around the world.

153

June 2

1 Peter 2:9–10

• • •

But you are a chosen race, a royal priesthood, a holy nation, God's own people, in order that you may proclaim the mighty acts of him who called you out of darkness into his marvelous light.

Once you were not a people,
but now you are God's people;
once you had not received mercy,
but now you have received mercy.

• • •

You are part of a royal family, you and your faith community. Look around you and see where you witness people carrying themselves with the dignity of kings and queens. This royal family has nothing to do with blood and has everything to do with openness. Your openness to my abundant love and grace is what ties you together, that and your commitment to sharing the good news of my grace with every person who is ready to know forgiveness and compassion and embrace. Today I invite you to see the ways in which you are part of this royal legacy and consider how you can extend that legacy to others.

June 3

Exodus 13:17–18a

• • •

When Pharaoh let the people go, God did not lead them by way of the land of the Philistines, although that was nearer; for God thought, "If the people face war, they may change their minds and return to Egypt." So God led the people by the roundabout way of the wilderness toward the Red Sea.

• • •

One of my beloved children once said, "It didn't take 40 years in the wilderness to get the Israelites out of Egypt; it took 40 years in the wilderness to get Egypt out of the Israelites." Generations of people who were enslaved in Egypt had internalized messages about their value and capacity; it took many years and a generation living and dying in the wilderness for them to reconnect with the inner spark I had placed in them. Today I invite you to reflect on a struggle in your life that took a long time. How did it prepare you to take on challenges later that you might not have been equipped for otherwise? I am so proud of you and your resilience. It will help you lead your people from the wilderness into new places.

June 4

2 Peter 1:10-11

• • •

Therefore, brothers and sisters, be all the more eager to confirm your call and election, for if you do this, you will never stumble. For in this way, entry into the eternal kingdom of our Lord and Savior Jesus Christ will be richly provided for you.

• • •

A bumper sticker says, "Jesus is coming; look busy!" As silly as this might sound, I am moved when my children in recovery from addiction return to daily twelve-step meetings after a season of struggle. I am moved by my formerly incarcerated children and military veterans dealing with post-traumatic stress disorder who begin volunteering in part to make a difference and in part to keep themselves from falling into unhealthy patterns. People's actions do not determine their welcome into my heavenly realm—only my grace determines that—but your actions help you live a life of thriving and joy. Today I invite you to reflect on where your consistent practice of service helps keep you aligned more deeply with me, and to celebrate that practice.

June 5

Leviticus 19:35–36

• • •

You shall not cheat in measuring length, weight, or quantity. You shall have honest balances, honest weights, an honest ephah, and an honest hin: I am the LORD your God, who brought you out of the land of Egypt.

• • •

When you have known suffering and then experience freedom from suffering, it can open something up inside you. It can help you live a life with integrity, never cheating or exploiting, because so much suffering is born of cheating and exploiting. And yet even though my ancient law invited your ancestors to practice that integrity, sometimes the fear that had saturated them during their oppression carried into their lives after they experienced freedom. The same might be true of you. Today I invite you to reflect on where you struggle to live with integrity. I invite you to put that struggle in conversation with any challenges you have faced, and where your liberation from those challenges might have taught you the benefit of following my will with honesty and integrity. By doing this, you will know a freedom few truly know.

June 6

1 John 3:18–20

• • •

Little children, let us love, not in word or speech, but in truth and action. And by this we will know that we are from the truth and will reassure our hearts before him whenever our hearts condemn us; for God is greater than our hearts, and he knows everything.

• • •

You need not fear me. You need only live with love. And when you fail to do that, turn to me for comfort, reassurance, and guidance in doing better the next time. The dishonesty that costs the most is the lies my children tell themselves to justify unkind actions instead of acknowledging them, seeking forgiveness, and turning back to my way. Today I invite you to be fully honest with yourself, including the less beautiful things about you, so that in confessing your shortcomings and seeking to act differently in the future, you may grow closer and closer to me.

June 7

Numbers 10:29

• • •

Moses said to Hobab son of Reuel the Midianite, Moses' father-in-law, "We are setting out for the place of which the LORD said, 'I will give it to you'; come with us, and we will treat you well; for the LORD has promised good to Israel."

• • •

Moses modeled something that my people sometimes repeated to my delight, but often failed to do, to my great sadness. Moses said to a people who were not of his immediate bloodline, a people who were not of his religion, that because of their faithfulness to the Israelites, they were part of the family. Who are the people in your life who your faith community keeps at arm's length? Who would be well served by a dose of my love and compassion? Reflect today on what it would look like to welcome them in.

June 8

2 John 1:6

• • •

And this is love, that we walk according to his commandments; this is the commandment just as you have heard it from the beginning—you must walk in it.

• • •

Sometimes people misrepresent the story of my relationship with my people. They say that I was a harsh God of laws before Jesus, and then a gentle God of compassion after. But my commandments *were* compassion. In a world where power dictates what is right and wrong, I cast a different path for you, my treasured children: by placing me first, by treasuring family, by treating others well, by living in gratitude for what you have instead of longing for what others have, you would know life. My beloved child who wrote this book in the days after Jesus understood that having a path of integrity in a world that does not value integrity was one of my gifts. Today revisit my commandments and ask yourself how they might actually provide a path of liberation for you.

June 9

Deuteronomy 4:9

• • •

But take care and watch yourselves closely, so as neither to forget the things that your eyes have seen nor to let them slip from your mind all the days of your life; make them known to your children and your children's children.

• • •

Sometimes people carry pain or shame related to their story or the story of their predecessors. And yet the only way the next generation can grow is to hear the *whole* story of their parents. In trying to protect your children, you sometimes hinder their growth. This has been true for generations. The myth of the self-made man (or woman) is a result of people not wanting to share their vulnerability and need for help. Many of my children think they are failures when they turn to others for help, even though I created a world where you would have many opportunities to build each other up and not isolate yourselves. What is your story of vulnerability and liberation? Who needs to hear it so the next generation can be more free?

June 10

3 John 1:5–6a

• • •

Beloved, you do faithfully whatever you do for the friends, even though they are strangers to you; they have testified to your love before the church.

• • •

My beloved child who wrote this passage had never heard the saying "a stranger is just a friend you haven't met yet," but this writer knew that in me, everyone is family. Hospitality, compassion, and generosity are brave gestures in this day and age, and yet they are also how you let the world know who I am. Today ask yourself how you can represent me in the world simply through an act of compassion for a stranger.

June 11

Joshua 20:1-3

• • •

Then the LORD spoke to Joshua, saying, "Say to the Israelites, 'Appoint the cities of refuge, of which I spoke to you through Moses, so that anyone who kills a person without intent or by mistake may flee there; they shall be for you a refuge from the avenger of blood.'"

• • •

My beloved child Gandhi is famous for saying "an eye for an eye makes the whole world blind," and my Son Jesus famously repudiated the teaching of an eye for an eye. In those early days I was trying to *curb* the mob bloodlust that often meted out punishment that was worse than the crime. And yet even then I wanted to help cast a different path—a path of potential healing when people do wrong and seek to be reconciled to those they wronged and to the community. Today you call that restorative justice. I invite you to explore how that part of my vision could be made to thrive in your own community.

June 12

Jude 1:22-23

• • •

And have mercy on some who are wavering; save others by snatching them out of the fire; and have mercy on still others with fear, hating even the tunic defiled by their bodies.

• • •

I ask you to extend compassion, provide paths to liberation, and protect those at risk of falling prey to temptation. And yet I do not ask you to let your body or soul be harmed by those of my children who function out of malice or cruelty. While I seek the salvation of all my children, I do not sacrifice one for another. If someone's actions harm you or others, you can tell them, and you can love and forgive them from a distance. In a healthy community, you can find others to work with them on their redemption and potentially their containment so they do not harm others. Today reflect on whether there are people in your life doing you real psychic, physical, or emotional harm. Seek help in creating healthy distance from them, placing your trust in me to save them in this life or the next.

June 13

Judges 10:11–14

· · ·

And the LORD said to the Israelites, "Did I not deliver you from the Egyptians and from the Amorites, from the Ammonites and from the Philistines? The Sidonians also, and the Amalekites, and the Maonites, oppressed you; and you cried to me, and I delivered you out of their hand. Yet you have abandoned me and worshiped other gods; therefore I will deliver you no more. Go and cry to the gods whom you have chosen; let them deliver you in the time of your distress."

· · ·

Free will means you get to choose your own path. It does not mean you are free of the consequences of your actions. And I am abundant in compassion and forgiveness, but there is a point at which that no longer helps you grow and thrive. I gave my beloved children a taste of what it was like to be in the world without me when they forgot to make me first in their lives. Their new gods did not show up, and we were again reconciled, but it also helped them realize the cost of not honoring me. Today I invite you to reflect on anything you have put ahead of me in your life, and what it has cost you in terms of your thriving.

June 14

Revelation 3:15–17

• • •

"I know your works; you are neither cold nor hot. I wish that you were either cold or hot. So, because you are lukewarm, and neither cold nor hot, I am about to spit you out of my mouth. For you say, 'I am rich, I have prospered, and I need nothing.' You do not realize that you are wretched, pitiable, poor, blind, and naked."

• • •

The "both sides," inclusive-of-all politics-churches worship a God of neutrality. But on some level neutrality is a myth, and the pursuit of neutrality can be the tool that keeps the existing, unjust powers in place by putting their agenda on equal footing with mine. I am not a neutral God. I show up over and over for those who are oppressed and who suffer. Meet me there, not in the middle.

June 15

Ruth 2:8–9

• • •

Then Boaz said to Ruth, "Now listen, my daughter, do not go to glean in another field or leave this one, but keep close to my young women. Keep your eyes on the field that is being reaped, and follow behind them. I have ordered the young men not to bother you. If you get thirsty, go to the vessels and drink from what the young men have drawn."

• • •

I am moved by Boaz's instinct to protect my beloved daughter Ruth although she was a foreigner whom many held in contempt for that reason alone. And I am sad he had to protect her. I know that she and her mother-in-law Naomi had to strategize for him to fall in love with Ruth so that both women could survive in a world that was cruel to widows. Today I invite you to pray fervently for a world where women—particularly women outside the mainstream (immigrants, trans women, sex workers)—do not need protectors like Boaz because this world is safe for women. And I ask you to pray for all the Boazes out there to show up over and over to help build that world alongside you.

June 16

Matthew 4:1–4

• • •

Then Jesus was led up by the Spirit into the wilderness to be tempted by the devil. He fasted for forty days and forty nights, and afterwards he was famished. The tempter came and said to him, "If you are the Son of God, command these stones to become loaves of bread." But he answered, "It is written,
'One does not live by bread alone,
　　but by every word that comes from the mouth of God.'"

• • •

One of my beloved children, a rabbi, once said, "When the devil wants to tempt you, it will not be to do something evil. It will be to do something good in the wrong way or at the wrong time." Often temptation is something that edges into human lives a little at a time, seemingly innocuous, sometimes even seeming to be a less-than-perfect means to a good end. Today I invite you to see where your hunger might make turning stones into bread very appealing. How can you, like my Son, use me and my word as a barrier to protect yourself from living outside of your relationship with me?

June 17

1 Samuel 3:12–13

• • •

On that day I will fulfill against Eli all that I have spoken concerning his house, from beginning to end. For I have told him that I am about to punish his house forever, for the iniquity that he knew, because his sons were blaspheming God, and he did not restrain them.

• • •

My son Eli played an important role in helping Samuel recognize my voice calling him to his path as a prophet. That makes it so much more sad that he did not himself listen to my voice guiding him and his sons to a path of faith and integrity. Today I invite you to reflect on who in your own family needs a word of truth or compassion and what your role is in speaking that word of truth or compassion. I gave you to each other to love each other, and helping people live in integrity with me is part of love.

June 18

Mark 5:33–34

• • •

But the woman, knowing what had happened to her, came in fear and trembling, fell down before him, and told him the whole truth. He said to her, "Daughter, your faith has made you well; go in peace, and be healed of your disease."

• • •

People tried to keep my beloved and suffering daughter away from my Son—and away from themselves—because her bleeding made her unclean. Her reaching out to Jesus was a transgression against societal rules. Those rules also said she didn't deserve to be in public, or to be treated with dignity. She knew me well enough to know those rules were out of keeping with my spirit of healing and compassion. She broke some foundational rules in order to stand for her own dignity and her own thriving. And my Son honored that, publicly, in the sight of the rulemakers. What rules do you see that cause unjust harm to people, or tell them they do not deserve dignity or a path to thriving? How can we partner in rewriting or dismantling those rules?

June 19

2 Samuel 6:20b-22

• • •

But Michal the daughter of Saul came out to meet David, and said, "How the king of Israel honored himself today, uncovering himself today before the eyes of his servants' maids, as any vulgar fellow might shamelessly uncover himself!" David said to Michal, "It was before the LORD, who chose me in place of your father and all his household, to appoint me as prince over Israel, the people of the LORD, that I have danced before the LORD. I will make myself yet more contemptible than this, and I will be abased in my own eyes; but by the maids of whom you have spoken, by them I shall be held in honor."

• • •

My son David was so full of joy because I had blessed his community that as people carried the box with the Ten Commandments to its new home, he danced fervently and enthusiastically. He sacrificed offerings to me. He forgot to carry himself with the decorum of a king and instead became a joy-filled child lost in his love for me. And he did me great honor when he said his reputation mattered far less than his celebration of me. Are you willing to be viewed as outside the norm in order to live a life of joy and celebration with me?

Liberating Love
JUN

June 20

Luke 6:36

• • •

Be merciful, just as your Father is merciful.

• • •

Today I invite you to think of five people you see as merciful. Pray for wisdom on how to live more like them. Then think of five faith communities or organizations you see as merciful. Pray for how to help your own community become more like them. And finally think of five laws that you see as merciful. Pray for guidance in how to create a society governed more by laws of mercy than of cruelty.

June 21

1 Kings 3:25–27

• • •

The king said, "Divide the living boy in two; then give half to one, and half to the other." But the woman whose son was alive said to the king—because compassion for her son burned within her—"Please, my lord, give her the living boy; certainly do not kill him!" The other said, "It shall be neither mine nor yours; divide it." Then the king responded: "Give the first woman the living boy; do not kill him. She is his mother."

• • •

This is what people mean when they talk about the Wisdom of my son Solomon. He was not perfect, and he was often out of alignment with my will, which shows that intelligence is not enough by itself for a person to align themselves to my will. And yet this moment, so stark in its clarity, shows what it means to love self-sacrificially, and also what it means for power to recognize the power of this love and respond to it. If only all of Solomon's reign could have looked like that. Today I invite you to reflect on how you can honor the value of love and compassion in the places where you have power or influence.

June 22

John 6:15

• • •

When Jesus realized that they were about to come and take him by force to make him king, he withdrew again to the mountain by himself.

• • •

My Son resisted all efforts to fit him into a traditional model of being at the top of a hierarchy; He knew that from the earliest days I had warned my children that rulers were destined to become dictators and bow to the temptations of corruption and exploitation. He knew there was a better way, where all of my children are equally honored and valued, where the community discerns together how to allocate resources and care for those in need. Today I invite you to pray for a world where there are no kings and peasants, rulers and ruled, but pray instead for my Beloved Community to exist on earth as it does in heaven.

June 23

2 Kings 4:42–44

• • •

A man came from Baal-shalishah, bringing food from the first fruits to the man of God: twenty loaves of barley and fresh ears of grain in his sack. Elisha said, "Give it to the people and let them eat." But his servant said, "How can I set this before a hundred people?" So he repeated, "Give it to the people and let them eat, for thus says the LORD, 'They shall eat and have some left.'" He set it before them, they ate, and had some left, according to the word of the LORD.

• • •

Jesus was not the first of my children to feed multitudes with a small amount of food. In both instances a far greater miracle occurred, though, than the one people focus on. People often try to turn me into a magician engaging in parlor tricks. My miracles are far more profound. In that gathering people transcended their sense of fear and scarcity. One person said, "I brought some dates from home; I can share." Someone else offered almonds, and someone provided olives. Loaves of bread appeared that people had been holding back, and suddenly a little barley and grain turned into a feast for those gathered. Today I ask you to pray to believe in my abundance and to practice generosity as if there will be enough: live as if I am real and can be trusted. As you teach others to do the same, abundance will surround you.

June 24

Acts 7:51–53

• • •

"You stiff-necked people, uncircumcised in heart and ears, you are forever opposing the Holy Spirit, just as your ancestors used to do. Which of the prophets did your ancestors not persecute? They killed those who foretold the coming of the Righteous One, and now you have become his betrayers and murderers. You are the ones that received the law as ordained by angels, and yet you have not kept it."

• • •

When you follow rules (such as circumcision) but resist the values that underpin those rules (being a people committed to my law of love), it is as if you ignored the rule itself. You get to eavesdrop here on an argument between my faithful son Stephen and people who saw my Son Jesus as a threat to their way of life and their faith. But he is speaking to you also. Today I invite you to reflect on where you are following rules but ignoring the law of love that underpins all rules that are actually of me. How can you allow your heart and ears to be circumcised, or committed to living by my love?

June 25

1 Chronicles 21:17

• • •

And David said to God, "Was it not I who gave the command to count the people? It is I who have sinned and done very wickedly. But these sheep, what have they done? Let your hand, I pray, O Lord my God, be against me and against my father's house; but do not let your people be plagued!"

• • •

This is a moment when my son David showed that he truly understood me. For millennia, people have blamed natural disasters on me. To this day, storms and earthquakes and tsunamis are called "Acts of God." What is powerful about this moment between David and me is that he took responsibility for his sin and told me not to punish others for his actions. It was a moment of true spiritual humility and the kind of leadership I always longed for him to show. Today I invite you to reflect on how you can commit to taking responsibility for your own actions so that others do not suffer as a result.

Liberating Love
JUN

June 26

Romans 6:4

• • •

Therefore we have been buried with him by baptism into death,
so that, just as Christ was raised from the dead by the glory of
the Father, so we too might walk in newness of life.

• • •

When my beloved daughter Carrie Nation was asked
from whence came her fiery passion for ending
alcoholism in the United States, she said, "from the icy cold
waters of the river where I was baptized." Life after death
is a whole new thing. Today I invite you to reflect on your
baptism, and how you want your life to be a whole new
thing. How can you live in newness of life, having been
buried and risen anew?

June 27

2 Chronicles 24:20

• • •

Then the spirit of God took possession of Zechariah son of the priest Jehoiada; he stood above the people and said to them, "Thus says God: Why do you transgress the commandments of the Lord, so that you cannot prosper? Because you have forsaken the Lord, he has also forsaken you."

• • •

Humanity has two Achilles' heels: greed and fear. While my laws are designed to protect every person in the community and also to protect the community as a whole, it is always either fear or greed (both born of a belief that there is not enough for everyone) that leads my children astray. My son Zechariah's message is a reminder to you also: is your community invested in each other's thriving? If not, it comes at a cost to the whole community and to each member. Pray for discernment about how to live into the abundance of my vision for you.

June 28

1 Corinthians 6:12

• • •

"All things are lawful for me," but not all things are beneficial. "All things are lawful for me," but I will not be dominated by anything.

• • •

Sometimes the laws of your land are in conflict with my laws, and sometimes they are just inadequate. Buying cereal is legal. The mistreatment of workers who harvest the grain for that cereal is a violation of my law. Today reflect on how to better live in my law so that you can have the comfort of nesting closer to me.

June 29

Ezra 6:20b-22

• • •

So they killed the passover lamb for all the returned exiles, for their fellow priests, and for themselves. It was eaten by the people of Israel who had returned from exile, and also by all who had joined them and separated themselves from the pollutions of the nations of the land to worship the LORD, the God of Israel. With joy they celebrated the festival of unleavened bread seven days; for the LORD had made them joyful, and had turned the heart of the king of Assyria to them, so that he aided them in the work on the house of God, the God of Israel.

• • •

No food tastes so good as that shared with family and friends you love. No food tastes so good as the food prepared in freedom. My children had practiced the ritual of Passover for millennia after being free from enslavement in Egypt. But this time they ate on their own land after a generation in forced exile. Today I invite you to celebrate your ancestors' liberation from enslavement, your people's reconnection with the land of their spiritual ancestors. I invite you to eat a meal as if you are finally eating it with your spiritual family after generations in exile, returned to your spiritual home. How does that ritual connect you to other refugees, exiles, and enslaved people?

June 30

2 Corinthians 6:11–13

• • •

We have spoken frankly to you Corinthians; our heart is wide open to you. There is no restriction in our affections, but only in yours. In return—I speak as to children—open wide your hearts also.

• • •

For some of my children, withholding affection is the only power they have. This world does so much damage, and people develop tools to protect themselves from harm. And yet my love can only grow deeper and stronger in you if you open wide your heart. My son Paul wrote this to a whole community that was functioning out of fear. Today I invite you to pray about where your community's hearts are closed: to each other, to my teachings of love, to a community surrounding them. Pray for ways that I might be welcomed into your hearts, that your community may know the vibrant life free from fear that I want for you all.

July 1

Nehemiah 2:17–20a

• • •

Then I said to them, "You see the trouble we are in, how Jerusalem lies in ruins with its gates burned. Come, let us rebuild the wall of Jerusalem, so that we may no longer suffer disgrace." I told them that the hand of my God had been gracious upon me, and also the words that the king had spoken to me. Then they said, "Let us start building!" So they committed themselves to the common good. But when Sanballat the Horonite and Tobiah the Ammonite official, and Geshem the Arab heard of it, they mocked and ridiculed us, saying, "What is this that you are doing? Are you rebelling against the king?" Then I replied to them, "The God of heaven is the one who will give us success, and we his servants are going to start building."

• • •

Sometimes you will face the task of rebuilding from scratch, like my son Nehemiah when my children returned to Jerusalem after a generation in exile. And when you start, some people will try to undermine you; they may tell you you're thinking too highly of yourself, that they know who you really are, that you're trying to defy the rules society has placed on you, like Sanballat et al. told Nehemiah. When that moment happens, remember that I am invested in your thriving and your faithfulness, and naysayers do not matter.

July 2

Galatians 3:1-2

• • •

You foolish Galatians! Who has bewitched you? It was before your eyes that Jesus Christ was publicly exhibited as crucified! The only thing I want to learn from you is this: Did you receive the Spirit by doing the works of the law or by believing what you heard?

• • •

There is a saying among young activists today: "Your respectability will not save you." What they mean is that if the state has decided your group of people is dangerous, then your safety is at risk no matter how well-behaved you are. The same was true for my early followers. You know that I have said that your actions reflect your beliefs, but Paul was conveying to those early Christians that they had witnessed the profound faithfulness of my Son in the face of state violence, and if that had not changed their hearts, then their actions meant nothing. Today I invite you to pay attention to where my Spirit is whispering in your ear, that you might believe and be comforted.

July 3

Esther 3:2–3

• • •

And all the king's servants who were at the king's gate bowed down and did obeisance to Haman; for the king had so commanded concerning him. But Mordecai did not bow down or do obeisance. Then the king's servants who were at the king's gate said to Mordecai, "Why do you disobey the king's command?"

• • •

The book of Esther was written to my children of Israel as they settled back into life in their homeland under a foreign ruler, after generations in exile. Some of them were getting comfortable with their non-Jewish neighbors and picking up some of their beliefs. And so the story of Esther and her uncle Mordecai offered to my children a reminder of how to live in harmony with people of different beliefs while remaining true to me. Most nations worshiped their king among gods. My son Mordecai risked his life by staying faithful to me. What are the ways in which your daily life invites you to honor or prioritize others before me? Today I invite you to pray for my support as you remain in relation to the world around you while not losing your connection to me in the process.

July 4

Ephesians 3:20–21

• • •

Now to him who by the power at work within us is able to accomplish abundantly far more than all we can ask or imagine, to him be glory in the church and in Christ Jesus to all generations, for ever and ever. Amen.

• • •

My power is so great, if you will open yourself up to it. You are often encouraged to worship leaders or nations, to put your faith in self-help gurus and television preachers. Today I invite you to consider what it would feel like to open yourself up instead to my power in you, and all that I can accomplish in and through you.

July 5

Job 16:2-4

• • •

"I have heard many such things;
    miserable comforters are you all.
Have windy words no limit?
    Or what provokes you that you keep on talking?
I also could talk as you do,
    if you were in my place;
I could join words together against you,
    and shake my head at you."

• • •

My poor son Job not only had to deal with the loss of all he held dear; he had to deal with friends who were more interested in lecturing than in supporting. Sometimes when my children try to fix each other's problems, they do more harm than good. Today I invite you to reflect on how you can share my love with your friends by doing more listening and extending compassion.

July 6

Philippians 2:5-8

• • •

Let the same mind be in you that was in Christ Jesus,
who, though he was in the form of God,
    did not regard equality with God
    as something to be exploited,
but emptied himself,
    taking the form of a slave,
    being born in human likeness.
And being found in human form,
    he humbled himself
    and became obedient to the point of death—
    even death on a cross.

• • •

True humility requires recognizing and trusting the divine spark I placed in you: trusting it so much that you do not need accolades or recognition in order to know your worth. My Son knew his true nature, which allowed him to live a life of justice, compassion, and service. Today seek that divine spark within, and seek a way to be of service that feels like Christlike humility rather than seeking recognition or praise from others. Allow me to affirm you, possibly in ways you might not expect.

July 7

Psalms 71:17–19

• • •

O God, from my youth you have taught me,
    and I still proclaim your wondrous deeds.
So even to old age and grey hairs,
    O God, do not forsake me,
until I proclaim your might
    to all the generations to come.
Your power and your righteousness, O God,
    reach the high heavens.

• • •

I am on this journey with you, from your birth to your last day. No matter the span of your life, I will keep showing up, encouraging, nudging you onward. Do not be ashamed of me; share my love. Let people know that the reason for your compassion, the reason for your generosity, the reason you fight for justice, is all because I extended compassion and generosity and will always fight for you.

July 8

Colossians 4:5-6

• • •

Conduct yourselves wisely toward outsiders, making the most of the time. Let your speech always be gracious, seasoned with salt, so that you may know how you ought to answer everyone.

• • •

The church in Colossae struggled with wanting to honor people who didn't worship Jesus while still staying true to their own beliefs and practices. My children today could learn a lot from what this letter reminded them: to treat everyone in a way that reflects grace and is rich in flavor, and to remember that if I have called you to engage wisely with people who aren't part of your community, you should do likewise with your own family, even in the midst of disagreement and tension. Today reflect on how your community's treatment of those around you could reflect my values of grace and preservation.

July 9

Proverbs 20:3

• • •

It is honorable to refrain from strife,
 but every fool is quick to quarrel.

• • •

Conflict can bring growth and healing and should not always be avoided, but conflict can be done in ways that foster enmity or ways that foster community.

Today I simply invite you to reflect on the places where the world would have put you in conflict with someone but you found a way to resolve that conflict in a healthy way. Reflect on the way my Spirit was with you. Offer a prayer of gratitude to me and invite my Spirit into all of your interactions. I made you to be a Healer of conflict—within yourself, between yourself and others, and in your whole community.

July 10

1 Thessalonians 5:1-2

• • •

Now concerning the times and the seasons, brothers and sisters, you do not need to have anything written to you. For you yourselves know very well that the day of the Lord will come like a thief in the night.

• • •

For millennia my children have wasted time trying to determine when I will return. Cults have risen and fallen around this same obsession. And the cost of it is great: in focusing on a future you cannot know, you miss all the ways that I was present throughout all of history, and even more importantly you miss all the ways I am right here in your midst, poised to help you build my realm on earth here and now. Today I invite you to pray to recognize that the day of the Lord is now, and pray for guidance for what to do in this day.

July 11

Ecclesiastes 4:1, 4

• • •

Again I saw all the oppressions that are practiced under the sun. Look, the tears of the oppressed—with no one to comfort them! On the side of their oppressors there was power—with no one to comfort them... Then I saw that all toil and all skill in work come from one person's envy of another. This also is vanity and a chasing after wind.

• • •

My beloved child wrote Ecclesiastes almost 2,500 years ago. And for all of human history, my heart has broken at this truth remaining the same: humanity uses power to exploit others for personal gain. Which means that for thousands of years, my children have misunderstood what power really is: power is being in relationship with each other, building a community where all your needs are met and all your gifts are honored. Anything else is vanity and chasing after wind. Any other power is ephemeral. Today I invite you to pray for an end to this corrupt power held by a handful of individuals and for it to be replaced with my lasting power that exists wherever community gathers to support and strengthen each other.

July 12

2 Thessalonians 2:9-10

• • •

The coming of the lawless one is apparent in the working of Satan, who uses all power, signs, lying wonders, and every kind of wicked deception for those who are perishing, because they refused to love the truth and so be saved.

• • •

Sometimes people joke, "the smartest thing Satan ever did was convince people he doesn't exist." Evil runs rampant in this world; people believe the lie that they need to be cruel in order to survive, to get ahead, to beat the competition. They believe the lie that other people *are* their competition. Today I invite you to pray that the evil and lies in your community, your nation, and your world would yield to the power of my truth. Pray that humanity might discover the truth of living in my love and thus be saved.

July 13

Song of Solomon 1:15–16a

• • •

Ah, you are beautiful, my love;
    ah, you are beautiful;
    your eyes are doves.
Ah, you are beautiful, my beloved,
    truly lovely.

• • •

Some people see this book as a romance between two of my children. Some see it as a story about Jesus and the church. Some say it is about my abundant love for my children of Israel. And all of these are beautiful ways of reading this book if it draws you closer to each other and closer to me. I celebrate the passion between my children as a connection between the divine spark in each of you. I celebrate my millennia-long relationship with my beloved Jewish children. I celebrate how my Son shows up to hold my church in a loving embrace. Today I invite you to lift up a prayer that celebrates love in all its forms, in any form that does not damage the heart and soul of either recipient. And I invite you to know that you are beautiful, truly lovely.

July 14

1 Timothy 4:12

• • •

Let no one despise your youth, but set the believers an example in speech and conduct, in love, in faith, in purity.

• • •

People sometimes mistake age for maturity, but some of my most faithful—and mature—followers are young in years. At every age, you have gifts that your community needs. Today I invite you to pause and reflect on your seasons of life—childhood, youth, young adulthood, middle age, eldership—and honor the ways that I have worked through you in each season. Offer a prayer of gratitude for the gifts I gave you in each season, and reflect on how in this season you can be an example in speech and conduct, in love, in faith, in purity.

July 15

Isaiah 43:8–9

• • •

Bring forth the people who are blind, yet have eyes,
    who are deaf, yet have ears!
Let all the nations gather together,
    and let the peoples assemble.
Who among them declared this,
    and foretold to us the former things?
Let them bring their witnesses to justify them,
    and let them hear and say, "It is true."

• • •

Sometimes when my children do not conform to societal norms, their wisdom and gifts are ignored. This passage reminds you to pay attention to my children who are differently abled. And it reminds you to pay attention to the parts of you that society wants to hide—these parts may be the way I'm trying to speak through you. Honor the people around you who do not meet society's norms, and honor the parts of you that do not meet society's norms. They speak to my magnificence in ways that the dominant culture never will.

July 16

2 Timothy 2:11–13

• • •

The saying is sure:
If we have died with him, we will also live with him;
if we endure, we will also reign with him;
if we deny him, he will also deny us;
if we are faithless, he remains faithful—
    for he cannot deny himself.

• • •

Read that passage again, carefully. That last sentence is reminding you that Christ lives within you. No matter how far you wander, you carry my divine spark within you. You are called to community (notice how the passage was written in the plural), so you don't have to navigate your journey with Jesus alone. Today pray to better see the Christ within you. Write down, or say out loud to yourself, "Christ lives within me!" so you can really practice believing how glorious you are.

July 17

Jeremiah 29:11–14a

• • •

For surely I know the plans I have for you, says the Lord, plans for your welfare and not for harm, to give you a future with hope. Then when you call upon me and come and pray to me, I will hear you. When you search for me, you will find me; if you seek me with all your heart, I will let you find me, says the Lord.

• • •

Today I invite you to read the first sentence again. And again. And again. Know that I mean every word. Know that I have plans for you, for your welfare and not for your harm. Know that I long for your thriving. And now read it knowing that I also mean it for your whole community. I have plans for your community's welfare and not for its harm. I long for your community's thriving. Today I simply ask that you call upon me and come and pray to me, knowing that I will hear you.

July 18

Titus 2:11–13

• • •

For the grace of God has appeared, bringing salvation to all, training us to renounce impiety and worldly passions, and in the present age to live lives that are self-controlled, upright, and godly, while we wait for the blessed hope and the manifestation of the glory of our great God and Savior, Jesus Christ.

• • •

My beloved child who wrote this passage gave you something of a math equation: I'm already here, and you are liberated. But also, live with discipline and hope for how my glory will show up in the future. And here is the thing: both are true. I am right here with you, calling on you to create heaven on earth right now, while I promise you will know my glory and my presence in the future. Today I invite you to see where I already am as well as where you want to see me soon.

July 19

Lamentations 2:13

• • •

What can I say for you, to what compare you,
    O daughter Jerusalem?
To what can I liken you, that I may comfort you,
    O virgin daughter Zion?
For vast as the sea is your ruin;
    who can heal you?

• • •

You already know that the city of Jerusalem and her many beloved inhabitants of many faiths have experienced so many risings and fallings in the millennia since my beloved servant wrote this passage. So many times the streets of Jerusalem have echoed with joy and laughter and prayers of praise. So many times the streets have echoed with screams of pain and moans of grief. And the same is true of your community. You have, collectively, known grief and joy and pain and praise. And in every season, I long either to celebrate with or to heal you. Today I invite you to read this passage again as if I am speaking it to your community. Of what shall I heal you?

July 20

Philemon 1:8-9a

• • •

For this reason, though I am bold enough in Christ to command you to do your duty, yet I would rather appeal to you on the basis of love.

• • •

Human notions of duty vary a lot from community to community. Reflect today on what "your duty" is as part of the body of Christ. And then reflect on what it means for you to live in ways that show your love. Are they the same? If not, which helps you find your way to me more readily? You might see why my beloved child who wrote Philemon expressed his frustration that the reader was failing in their duty, but he knew he needed to take a different approach. In all things, my precious, precious child, love. In every action you take, love. In that way, you will exceed any duty I could assign to you.

July 21

Ezekiel 18:21–23

• • •

But if the wicked turn away from all their sins that they have committed and keep all my statutes and do what is lawful and right, they shall surely live; they shall not die. None of the transgressions that they have committed shall be remembered against them; for the righteousness that they have done they shall live. Have I any pleasure in the death of the wicked, says the Lord God, and not rather that they should turn from their ways and live?

• • •

No matter how far my children stray from their path, it is always my deepest longing that they return. There is nothing I can't forgive. This is not a parlor game where people choose to live lives of horrendous greed and cruelty, knowing that they can ask for forgiveness at the last moment. No one knows when their last moment will be. But when my children seek to henceforth lead a new life in my light, I know an abundance of joy. Know that there is nothing you and I cannot reconcile. There is nothing you have done that needs to be held against you forever. Similarly, look around your community and notice who continues to be punished for crimes long past and repented. Ask how your community can show the same love to them.

July 22

James 2:1–4

• • •

My brothers and sisters, do you with your acts of favoritism really believe in our glorious Lord Jesus Christ? For if a person with gold rings and in fine clothes comes into your assembly, and if a poor person in dirty clothes also comes in, and if you take notice of the one wearing the fine clothes and say, "Have a seat here, please", while to the one who is poor you say, "Stand there", or, "Sit at my feet", have you not made distinctions among yourselves, and become judges with evil thoughts?

• • •

My way is simple but not easy. And in a world that values money and status, my way is also countercultural. Look around your community. Are the gifts of people who don't have high status valued in your community? Do they have the same positions of responsibility and authority? Are they helping shape the direction of your community? If not, then today I invite you to pray for guidance on how to help your community align better with my way. And if so, offer up prayers for diligence in staying on my path when the world so badly wants to pull you off of it.

July 23

Daniel 9:16–17

• • •

O Lord, in view of all your righteous acts, let your anger and wrath, we pray, turn away from your city Jerusalem, your holy mountain; because of our sins and the iniquities of our ancestors, Jerusalem and your people have become a disgrace among all our neighbors. Now therefore, O our God, listen to the prayer of your servant and to his supplication, and for your own sake, Lord, let your face shine upon your desolated sanctuary.

• • •

My son Daniel reflected deeply on the teachings of the prophet Jeremiah, praying for an end to my anger with Jerusalem for failing me again and again. Being a prophet is a hard task: calling on your people to do better and simultaneously calling on me to yet again be merciful. Who in your life needs to do better but also needs an advocate? Lift them up in prayer to me today, whether it be a person or a people. Use this passage as the template for your prayer and seek me fully today, on behalf of those imperfect souls in your life.

July 24

James 1:26-27

• • •

If any think they are religious, and do not bridle their tongues but deceive their hearts, their religion is worthless. Religion that is pure and undefiled before God, the Father, is this: to care for orphans and widows in their distress, and to keep oneself unstained by the world.

• • •

Working with widows and orphans in their distress might lead to moments of frustration and overwhelm some of my children, but some of my brilliance with this calling is that it will keep you grounded in what really matters: nothing keeps gossip and intrigue at bay like the work of helping your siblings survive in a world that does not help them do so. How might you be able to connect with me through the work that connects you to people in need? How might we grow closer through your standing with those who need me the most?

July 25

Hosea 7:8–10

• • •

Ephraim mixes himself with the peoples;
    Ephraim is a cake not turned.
Foreigners devour his strength,
    but he does not know it;
gray hairs are sprinkled upon him,
    but he does not know it.
Israel's pride testifies against him;
    yet they do not return to the LORD their God,
    or seek him, for all this.

• • •

Humility is such a bedrock for connection with me. In this passage, Hosea reminded the tribe of Ephraim that they could not see their limitations and challenges. Today I invite you to reflect on your own community and how you might humble yourselves so you can hear the ways to deepen your relationship with me and become a stronger community.

July 26

1 Peter 2:23-25

• • •

When he was abused, he did not return abuse; when he suffered, he did not threaten; but he entrusted himself to the one who judges justly. He himself bore our sins in his body on the cross, so that, free from sins, we might live for righteousness; by his wounds you have been healed. For you were going astray like sheep, but now you have returned to the shepherd and guardian of your souls.

• • •

My beloved Son was judged UNjustly by the powers and systems of the Roman Empire and by religious leaders who wielded their power in cruel ways. But he found strength in me when the world treated him cruelly for living compassionately and peacefully in the face of hatred and violence. Know that following my Son is not easy: this world does not embrace compassion—but some of my followers do. How will you find those who want to build this community where I guard your souls and you care for each other and my many sheep who have not received compassion?

July 27

Joel 2:28-29

• • •

Then afterward
    I will pour out my spirit on all flesh;
your sons and your daughters shall prophesy,
      your old men shall dream dreams,
      and your young men shall see visions.
Even on the male and female slaves,
      in those days, I will pour out my spirit.

• • •

When humankind fails to live out my call for all people to be free and to thrive, in those moments I pour out a blessing on them that they might participate in their own liberation. Fear and lack of vision have caused my children to do horrible things, and so my spirit moves among you, casting vision that you might dream bigger and build bigger. Listen today: my spirit is calling you out of fear and out of cruelty. My spirit is speaking through those this world has enslaved and discarded. What is she saying to you?

July 28

2 Peter 2:18-19

• • •

For they speak bombastic nonsense, and with licentious desires of the flesh they entice people who have just escaped from those who live in error. They promise them freedom, but they themselves are slaves of corruption; for people are slaves to whatever masters them.

• • •

In every generation are people who seek to use the language of my love for evil ends, to benefit themselves at the expense of my beloved children. Today I want you to reflect on the people in your life who might be prone to temptation but are seeking to live a life of faith in me. How might you help them get the support and love they need? How can your faith community bolster them? And reach out to me for the ways I can also bolster you in times when you are weary and prone to being tempted by those who offer false promises.

July 29

Amos 5:15

• • •

Hate evil and love good,
    and establish justice in the gate;
it may be that the Lᴏʀᴅ, the God of hosts,
    will be gracious to the remnant of Joseph.

• • •

One of my children once said, "justice is what love looks like in public." It pleases my heart when my children create systems that allow people to be treated with dignity and worth. I value charity, but I want for you a world where you do not have to rely on charity, because your community is governed by justice. Today I invite you to reflect on how your community could better establish justice, that I might be invited in to extend grace.

July 30

1 John 4:18-21

. . .

There is no fear in love, but perfect love casts out fear; for fear has to do with punishment, and whoever fears has not reached perfection in love. We love because he first loved us. Those who say, "I love God", and hate their brothers or sisters, are liars; for those who do not love a brother or sister whom they have seen, cannot love God whom they have not seen. The commandment we have from him is this: those who love God must love their brothers and sisters also.

. . .

Sometimes, I know, it is hard to love people because you fear them. If there is a sibling (one of my children) that you struggle to love, today I invite you to reflect on what it is about them that you fear. Turn that fear over to me. Practice today what it feels like to love them amidst all their sins and failings and imperfections. Notice whether you feel lighter in any way. Fear is a burden I seek to lift from you.

July 31

Obadiah:11–12

• • •

On the day that you stood aside,
  on the day that strangers carried off his wealth,
and foreigners entered his gates
  and cast lots for Jerusalem,
  you too were like one of them.
But you should not have gloated over your brother
  on the day of his misfortune;
you should not have rejoiced over the people of Judah
  on the day of their ruin;
you should not have boasted
  on the day of distress.

• • •

Rabbis tell a story about the day the Israelites escaped slavery. As the Egyptian soldiers drowned in the Red Sea as it closed, the angels danced in celebration, and I said, "My creations are drowning, and you dance before me?" Justice and consequences for wrong actions are necessary. And yet it is my hope you will never celebrate someone else's suffering, because in that moment you distance yourself from me. Today I invite you to reflect on what it means to be siblings with all of humanity, and how to practice that belief even with those who need to face consequences for their actions.

August

August 1

Jonah 4:2

• • •

He prayed to the LORD and said, "O LORD! Is not this what I said while I was still in my own country? That is why I fled to Tarshish at the beginning; for I knew that you are a gracious God and merciful, slow to anger, and abounding in steadfast love, and ready to relent from punishing."

• • •

My poor son and prophet Jonah. He did not want Tarshish to experience compassion, because what they had done hurt his people so badly. My grace is so hard for my children to understand, because it can feel like I do not care about their suffering as much as I care about the perpetrator's healing. Today I invite you to think of the ways I have extended grace to you, and what it means to receive my full compassion and desire for your wholeness. Then I invite you to imagine that I treasure you and every one of my children so much I want you all to know full reconciliation to me. What world can you and I create together where everyone gets to experience my grace?

August 2

2 John 1:8

• • •

Be on your guard, so that you do not lose what we have worked for, but may receive a full reward.

• • •

Temptation to take shortcuts, or to be less kind or loving or patient than you are supposed to be—will constantly surround you. I do not just offer heaven as an alternative. I offer a life where you receive compassion and support, where you are known in community, where your needs are met and your gifts are honored here and now. Today I ask you to be on your guard: look for the people who help you be your best self. Thank them for playing that role. They are there so you may receive a full reward.

August 3

Micah 5:7

• • •

Then the remnant of Jacob,
　　surrounded by many peoples,
shall be like dew from the LORD,
　　like showers on the grass,
which do not depend upon people
　　or wait for any mortal.

• • •

What some people don't notice about my prophets is that every single one ends their story, no matter how horrific, with a happy ending. If your community can align with my calling to be a people of compassion and justice, you will know such joy and you will feel such deep connection to me. My son Micah reminded a people whose community was coming unraveled because of their cruelty and indifference that a different world was possible. Today I invite you to dream about what your community can be when it is grounded in my love and compassion. Lift that vision up as a prayer to me so that we can be about that work together.

August 4

3 John 1:11

• • •

Beloved, do not imitate what is evil but imitate what is good. Whoever does good is from God; whoever does evil has not seen God.

• • •

My Son once said, "whoever is not against us is for us." In a world where people are suspicious of motives and strategies, I invite you to engage the people around you based on their actions more than the labels attached to them. Many people use my name for evil ends. Many people never use my name but do my will. I would rather you seek the latter than the former. Today I invite you to notice where I am showing up in the world and in your life, even if my name never is mentioned. Lift those places up to me in a prayer of gratitude, that I might rejoice in how you are being fed by the good that surrounds you.

August 5

Nahum 3:8, 10a

• • •

Are you better than Thebes
    that sat by the Nile,
with water around her,
    her rampart a sea,
    water her wall?
Yet she became an exile,
    she went into captivity.

• • •

For thousands of years people have preached the false message that if a nation is powerful, it is because I have blessed it. But how could I be seduced by power when I am the source of power? The only thing that is true is that every empire that exploited people and practiced cruelty has collapsed under its own weight. My blessing rains down on communities of compassion and care. Today I ask you to pray for nations that seem great but do evil, that they might find their way back to me, to compassion and care.

August 6

Jude 1:24-25

• • •

Now to him who is able to keep you from falling, and to make you stand without blemish in the presence of his glory with rejoicing, to the only God our Savior, through Jesus Christ our Lord, be glory, majesty, power, and authority, before all time and now and forever. Amen.

• • •

You are beautiful. You are glorious. You are strong. You are whole. When you come before me, I see who you truly are. Today I invite you to lean on me—to share with me the places you are shaky—so that I can support you, so that you can feel me keeping you from falling. And today I invite you to look into the mirror until you can see who you truly are, until you can see what I see when you come before me: your beautiful, compassionate, glorious self—made in my image.

August 7

Habakkuk 2:2–3

• • •

Then the LORD answered me and said:
Write the vision;
    make it plain on tablets,
    so that a runner may read it.
For there is still a vision for the appointed time;
    it speaks of the end, and does not lie.
If it seems to tarry, wait for it;
    it will surely come, it will not delay.

• • •

Your generation needs a billboard of hope. In a time where everyone is in constant motion, they need a big, simple, bold message that can penetrate the frenzy of daily life. Today I invite you to imagine the billboard you would create on my behalf, simple enough and big enough that a runner zipping by might read it. What word will we bring to your people, my beloved child?

August 8

Revelation 22:1-2

• • •

Then the angel showed me the river of the water of life, bright as crystal, flowing from the throne of God and of the Lamb through the middle of the street of the city. On either side of the river is the tree of life with its twelve kinds of fruit, producing its fruit each month; and the leaves of the tree are for the healing of the nations.

• • •

Imagine what this world will be like when all the nations are healed. Imagine how you will feel—what stresses will go away, what joy will be able to return to its fullness. This is what I want for you and for your neighbors and for your siblings in every land. Today I ask you to simply bask in the image of what this world will look like healed. I ask you to call forth the faces of mothers and fathers and children and grandparents in your community and in other communities ravaged by violence and war and poverty, and I ask you to pray that you and they might gain access to the leaves of the tree for the healing of the nations. Finally, imagine yourselves tending and nurturing that tree together, for my sake and for yours.

August 9

Zephaniah 2:3

• • •

Seek the LORD, all you humble of the land,
    who do his commands;
seek righteousness, seek humility;
    perhaps you may be hidden
    on the day of the LORD's wrath.

• • •

My beloved son Zephaniah's name means "Yahweh has hidden," and his book was a reminder to my children of Israel to follow my path of peace and justice in order to know safety and comfort, even if that path is not the most obvious and visible path. Living in arrogance and ignoring the work of justice guarantee an empty life, and Zephaniah knew I wanted more for you. Today I invite you to notice the humble people in your life and thank them for showing you a different way of being in a world saturated with aggression and self-aggrandizement.

August 10

Matthew 5:5

• • •

Blessed are the meek, for they will inherit the earth.

• • •

My beloved Son was quoting a long-held promise of mine from Psalm 37: "The meek shall inherit the land and delight themselves in abundant prosperity." In another translation, my Son's famous speech began "Blessed are the *gentle.*" When my children finally align with my will for peace and compassion and gentleness, this whole land will know thriving. You are part of my plan. Today reflect on the ways you are creating a culture of gentleness. Honor what you are already doing to bring my will to fulfillment. Know that I am encouraged by you and I see what you are doing to heal this nation and make it a place where the meek know and feel my blessing.

August 11

Haggai 2:6-7

• • •

For thus says the LORD of hosts: Once again, in a little while, I will shake the heavens and the earth and the sea and the dry land; and I will shake all the nations, so that the treasure of all nations shall come, and I will fill this house with splendor, says the LORD of hosts.

• • •

When my children returned from their captivity, they knew how beautiful Solomon's temple had once been, and they were not excited about building something that would be inferior. My beloved child Haggai reminded them that their act of seeking to honor me would be enough, and the glory of this new temple would be breathed into the space by my presence. Today some spaces of worship look worn and beleaguered. Know that I can make any space gleam so long as the people in it are doing my work of kindness and service and love. Reflect on how your own worshiping community can reflect my love to a people in need of love.

August 12

Mark 8:34–35

• • •

He called the crowd with his disciples, and said to them, "If any want to become my followers, let them deny themselves and take up their cross and follow me. For those who want to save their life will lose it, and those who lose their life for my sake, and for the sake of the gospel, will save it."

• • •

A question my children have begun asking each other in this generation brings me joy: "Do you want to survive, or do you want to thrive?" My Son reminded his followers that the effort of protecting oneself from potential harm costs people the chance of really exploring the beauty of this world and all the people in it. By taking risks, by living for others, by pursuing a life like that of my Son, generations have found freedom and joy that they never would have if they had sought simply to survive. How will you take a risk, be vulnerable, live for others, and follow my Son today so that you may actually thrive and live life abundantly?

August 13

Zechariah 10:6

• • •

I will strengthen the house of Judah,
and I will save the house of Joseph.
I will bring them back because I have compassion on them,
and they shall be as though I had not rejected them;
for I am the LORD their God and I will answer them.

• • •

Every story in your sacred scriptures is ultimately a story with the possibility of a happy ending, including the prophetic books. I am a God of second and seventh and seven times seventy chances, not just for individuals but for whole families and neighborhoods and cultures and nations. What will your faith community look like when it has humbled itself and fully aligned itself with me so that I might be allowed to share my compassion with you all? Pray today for that turning to happen in your own community, that it might be strengthened by my even deeper presence within it.

August 14

Luke 6:49

• • •

"But the one who hears and does not act is like a man who built a house on the ground without a foundation. When the river burst against it, immediately it fell, and great was the ruin of that house."

• • •

Knowing a thing and practicing a thing are very different from each other. Your brain internalizes and normalizes that which you practice. What will you choose to enact today so that it might become part of you and give you a stronger foundation? I want this for you so that when harder times come, you will not be washed away by the tides of evil rulers or pernicious people trying to pull you from my ways of peace and love.

August 15

Malachi 3:6–7a

• • •

For I the LORD do not change; therefore you, O children of Jacob, have not perished. Ever since the days of your ancestors you have turned aside from my statutes and have not kept them. Return to me, and I will return to you, says the LORD of hosts.

• • •

A strange narrative about me makes the rounds every so often: the angry, vengeful God of the Hebrew Bible versus the kind, compassionate God of the New Testament. But throughout all of human history I have remained steadfast, a God of love and compassion and also a God of justice. Today I make you the same promise I made to the early church, to the people of Israel, to the remnant of Judah, to Abraham, and to Adam and Eve: return to me, and I will return to you. Know that I will always be there whenever you are ready, whenever you are in need, whenever you seek my comfort, compassion, and grace.

August 16

John 7:52

• • •

They replied, "Surely you are not also from Galilee, are you?
Search and you will see that no prophet is to arise from Galilee."

• • •

No matter how many times I choose the sex worker, the second son, the shepherd plucked from obscurity, my children always seek leaders from the halls of power, people who "look" like leaders, people with the right pedigree. And yet I seek to build for and with you a community grounded in humility and compassion and inclusion for all, so over and over I give you gifted leaders and prophets and preachers and even a savior from "the wrong side of the tracks." Today I invite you to look for the places where my gospel is being enacted by people who don't come from the halls of power or from prominent institutions, but come from down the hill or down the block or from a rough neighborhood. Seek me and honor me there.

August 17

Genesis 33:4

• • •

But Esau ran to meet him, and embraced him, and fell on his neck and kissed him, and they wept.

• • •

I long for the reconciliation of my children to one another. Both of my sons Esau and Jacob lived with the ramifications of bad choices their father (and mother) made, and ultimately they found ways to reconnect and heal the rift that had been imposed on them. My heart danced that day. Today I invite you to reflect on whether there is any rift you need to heal, and invite me to be present as you work toward that goal.

August 18

Acts 8:36–38

• • •

As they were going along the road, they came to some water; and the eunuch said, "Look, here is water! What is to prevent me from being baptized?" He commanded the chariot to stop, and both of them, Philip and the eunuch, went down into the water, and Philip baptized him.

• • •

One of the reasons I treasure my beloved son Philip so much is that no matter where he ended up, he did not try to limit who I could love and who could love me. Men of power and influence, women who were not valued by the world, whole families of people as well as people with no families are all deserving of a chance to experience newness, which is what baptism is all about. This was true for my Jewish children and for the followers of John the Baptist and followers of my Son Jesus. Today I invite you to reflect on who in your life needs my love and faces barriers to receiving it. How might you share a chance at newness with them?

August 19

Exodus 22:25-27

• • •

If you lend money to my people, to the poor among you, you shall not deal with them as a creditor; you shall not exact interest from them. If you take your neighbor's cloak in pawn, you shall restore it before the sun goes down; for it may be your neighbor's only clothing to use as cover; in what else shall that person sleep? And if your neighbor cries out to me, I will listen, for I am compassionate.

• • •

How I wish you children could understand my fervent desire that you not exploit each other's struggles and suffering. Today I ask you to imagine what your world might look like if you were all able to slow down enough to learn the cause of people's debts and sufferings and find a way forward that would not result in people ending up back in the hard place where they started.

August 20

Romans 7:15

• • •

I do not understand my own actions. For I do not do what I want, but I do the very thing I hate.

• • •

My children so often work against their own best interests. They get seduced by easy fixes that end up being hard. They know what is right and do what is wrong anyhow. I made your mind strong, but I made your heart stronger, so that the wisdom of your heart might persevere. Today I want to remind you that I love you even when you do that which you hate, and I stand with you all the time so that you might practice more and more every day doing that which I love.

August 21

Leviticus 19:18

• • •

You shall not take vengeance or bear a grudge against any of your people, but you shall love your neighbor as yourself: I am the LORD.

• • •

Who bears you a grudge? Would your life be lighter if they followed this teaching? Long before my Son reminded my children of this teaching, my children starting a new life in a new land with new laws were taught to love their neighbor as themselves. I ask this of you not just because you experience lightness when you receive grace, but because you experience lightness when you extend grace. I ask you to do it because you know that my will is for your thriving. I ask you to do it so you can know true freedom.

August 22

1 Corinthians 9:25

• • •

Athletes exercise self-control in all things; they do it to receive a perishable wreath, but we an imperishable one.

• • •

M y children in the church in ancient Corinth needed some help with self-control—and so do many of my children. Some of my children practice discipline so they can die and kill for a country. Some practice discipline so they can receive trophies. But when you practice self-control in community, you contribute to building my realm on earth—a realm where all needs are met and all gifts are honored. How might your self-discipline contribute to your community?

August 23

Numbers 11:10–12

• • •

Moses heard the people weeping throughout their families, all at the entrances of their tents. Then the LORD became very angry, and Moses was displeased. So Moses said to the LORD, "Why have you treated your servant so badly? Why have I not found favor in your sight, that you lay the burden of all this people on me? Did I conceive all this people? Did I give birth to them, that you should say to me, 'Carry them in your bosom, as a nurse carries a sucking child, to the land that you promised on oath to their ancestors?'"

• • •

My most faithful servants do not always have the easiest jobs. The people of Israel were so afraid, and fearful people act badly. My son Moses so often felt trapped between their bad behavior and my frustration with their ingratitude. And yet he knew the radiance of my love like few have. Leading my people can be lonely but it can draw us closer. What costs would you be willing to take on in order to do my will for your people, no matter how ungrateful they may be?

August 24

2 Corinthians 8:9–11

• • •

For you know the generous act of our Lord Jesus Christ, that though he was rich, yet for your sakes he became poor, so that by his poverty you might become rich.

• • •

The writer of this letter understood metaphors, didn't he? My Son's riches were not gold and rubies. His poverty was literal, to show you there are other ways to be rich. And the riches you receive in following me are also not rubies or gold—any who say that they are has misunderstood my Son's teachings. Today I ask you to reflect on what my Son's literal poverty—simple living, without wealth or even permanent shelter—offers you as a lesson for how to live a life oriented around true riches.

August 25

Deuteronomy 4:31

• • •

Because the LORD your God is a merciful God, he will neither abandon you nor destroy you; he will not forget the covenant with your ancestors that he swore to them.

• • •

I promised many generations ago that I would never leave your side. You and your people belong to me, and that goes for all groups of people, no matter how distant they feel from me. Today I invite you to picture your people in every configuration. Picture me holding you all close. Picture me offering comfort to you all. Picture me guiding you all toward a better life together. Know that those pictures are real.

August 26

Galatians 4:13-14

• • •

You know that it was because of a physical infirmity that I first announced the gospel to you; though my condition put you to the test, you did not scorn or despise me, but welcomed me as an angel of God, as Christ Jesus.

• • •

My son Paul really understood that my power looks nothing like human power, which has always made it so hard for humans to fully trust. I show up alongside the people whom this world rejects. My power is made manifest through a people who had been enslaved by a cruel empire. My power is made manifest through a woman whom I made a judge over men in a time when women had no power. My power is made manifest through my Son who was murdered by a government because his message of love and inclusion was such a threat to their rule of tyranny and conquest. And my power was made manifest in the early church through the teachings of a man with a disability who did not hide himself or his disability but said, "If you embrace me in my weakness, you embrace God, who is building a movement of people who are weak by the world's standards but strong in compassion and love, which is real power." Today I invite you to ask whether and how you hide your vulnerabilities, and I invite you to pray for help finding the community that will care for you as the Galatians cared for Paul.

August 27

Joshua 22:26–27

• • •

Therefore we said, "Let us now build an altar, not for burnt offering, nor for sacrifice, but to be a witness between us and you, and between the generations after us, that we do perform the service of the LORD in his presence with our burnt offerings and sacrifices and offerings of well-being; so that your children may never say to our children in time to come, "You have no portion in the LORD."

• • •

What moves me about this scripture is that my children so long ago knew that the purpose of ritual isn't to appease me. The purpose of ritual is to remind the community of their relationship with me. As you pass those rituals down to your children, take care that they know this isn't about superstition or habit. Every time you participate together in any sort of act that honors me, you are saying to each other and to your children, "we are a people in relationship with our loving God." I invite you to be intentional with your rituals so they do not lose their connection to their true purpose.

August 28

Ephesians 4:11–12

• • •

The gifts he gave were that some would be apostles, some prophets, some evangelists, some pastors and teachers, to equip the saints for the work of ministry, for building up the body of Christ.

• • •

What a boring world you would inhabit if everyone were the same, with the same gifts and the same skills. I wish that my children knew that every gift is equally sacred, that all work honors me. Today I invite you to think about who in your community shares gifts that aren't as valued as the flashier, more noticeable ones. Take a moment to tell them you see the gifts I placed in them and that you appreciate them.

August 29

Judges 11:1-2

• • •

Now Jephthah the Gileadite, the son of a prostitute, was a mighty warrior. Gilead was the father of Jephthah. Gilead's wife also bore him sons; and when his wife's sons grew up, they drove Jephthah away, saying to him, "You shall not inherit anything in our father's house; for you are the son of another woman."

• • •

If you have read the book of Judges, you know how important Jephthah was to my people. What you may not know is how treasured his mother, a prostitute, was to me. My children have always been cruel to people with limited options, whether it is because they are afraid of life becoming that hard for them, or because life is already so hard for them that their only solace is looking down on someone else. Today I invite you to reflect on who the undervalued people are in your midst—those like Jephthah or Jephthah's mother. Let them know I love them and that they are called to great things.

August 30

Philippians 2:14–15

• • •

Do all things without murmuring and arguing, so that you may be blameless and innocent, children of God without blemish in the midst of a crooked and perverse generation, in which you shine like stars in the world.

• • •

Often my children seek to follow this teaching by suppressing their frustrations and sense of resentment, but that simply poisons good people. What I call you into instead is a sense of your relationship with me that allows you to release resentments, speak honestly about things that have genuinely hurt you, and not be attached to outcomes that you cannot control. I want for you peace and ease even as you do challenging things. Today I invite you to ponder what life would feel like if you did not have to suppress frustration and resentment, and to ponder also how to create that reality in your community.

August 31

Ruth 2:20

• • •

Then Naomi said to her daughter-in-law, "Blessed be he by the LORD, whose kindness has not forsaken the living or the dead!" Naomi also said to her, "The man is a relative of ours, one of our nearest kin."

• • •

When Ruth and her mother-in-law had no resources in a world that barely pretended to care for widows, Naomi's relative Boaz cared for her without fully realizing he was caring for family. Imagine a world where compassion is our first instinct when we see people in need, rather than suspicion. My hope for you is that you may encounter many Boazes in your hard moments and that you might be Boaz to many in need.

September

Liberating Love

SEP

365 LOVE NOTES FROM GOD

· September 1 ·

1 Samuel 8:6-8

• • •

But the thing displeased Samuel when they said, "Give us a king to govern us." Samuel prayed to the LORD, and the LORD said to Samuel, "Listen to the voice of the people in all that they say to you; for they have not rejected you, but they have rejected me from being king over them. Just as they have done to me, from the day I brought them up out of Egypt to this day, forsaking me and serving other gods, so also they are doing to you.

• • •

When my children got tired of listening to my guidance, they sought judges. When the judges also gave them a different path than the nations around them, they called for a king. My beloved child, rarely does my path point you in the direction of others. My children many years ago could not manage to stand alone on a different path than those around them. How will you weather the challenges of following my path when it veers from the culture around you?

September 2

Colossians 3:1-2

• • •

So if you have been raised with Christ, seek the things that are above, where Christ is, seated at the right hand of God. Set your minds on things that are above, not on things that are on earth.

• • •

My children so often seek the path of least resistance. But lack of resistance rarely leads to resurrection. By comparing yourself to those around you, you will never reach great heights. By focusing on my Son, your vision will always be pointed toward what matters. Today I long for you to know that I want for you far more than the world can offer. You deserve things that are above.

September 3

2 Samuel 7:18–19

• • •

Then King David went in and sat before the LORD, and said, "Who am I, O Lord GOD, and what is my house, that you have brought me thus far? And yet this was a small thing in your eyes, O Lord GOD; you have spoken also of your servant's house for a great while to come. May this be instruction for the people, O Lord GOD!"

• • •

I remember so fondly my son David in the days when he was a humble and faithful servant who as a result was brought to lofty positions. How I wish he could have remained so, and thus been the model of leadership I want for my beloved children. Today I invite you to reflect on your own journey and where you have felt my presence. Your practice of gratitude not only honors me, it heals you.

September 4

1 Thessalonians 5:9-11

• • •

For God has destined us not for wrath but for obtaining salvation through our Lord Jesus Christ, who died for us, so that whether we are awake or asleep we may live with him. Therefore encourage one another and build up each other, as indeed you are doing.

• • •

I want you to feel encouraged and built up. I treasure you so much and hope for you to be in a community where each of you knows your value in my eyes because you encourage each other. In this way you can experience a taste of heaven. Today I invite you to encourage someone in your midst and also let someone know that you could use some encouragement.

September 5

1 Kings 8:41–43

• • •

"Likewise when a foreigner, who is not of your people Israel, comes from a distant land because of your name—for they shall hear of your great name, your mighty hand, and your outstretched arm—when a foreigner comes and prays toward this house, then hear in heaven your dwelling-place, and do according to all that the foreigner calls to you, so that all the peoples of the earth may know your name and fear you, as do your people Israel, and so that they may know that your name has been invoked on this house that I have built."

• • •

My beloved son Solomon offered this prayer to me when he blessed his temple, but he was also instructing his people that honoring the stranger was a sacred act, and it was how the world would know of my love. When a foreigner arrives in your community, do they experience my love? Today I invite you to pray about how my children from every corner of the world might encounter me through your community's welcome.

September 6

2 Thessalonians 2:16–17

• • •

Now may our Lord Jesus Christ himself and God our Father, who loved us and through grace gave us eternal comfort and good hope, comfort your hearts and strengthen them in every good work and word.

• • •

My children, including you, deserve to know that I am with you from the beginning of time to its end. This text reminds you my love is for whole communities and not just individuals, but today I want you to take a moment simply to experience the deep love I have for you and the deep desire I have for your every good work and word. Beloved, you are loved.

September 7

2 Kings 5:11-14

• • •

But Naaman became angry and went away, saying, "I thought that for me he would surely come out, and stand and call on the name of the LORD his God, and would wave his hand over the spot, and cure the leprosy! Are not Abana and Pharpar, the rivers of Damascus, better than all the waters of Israel? Could I not wash in them, and be clean?" He turned and went away in a rage. But his servants approached and said to him, "Father, if the prophet had commanded you to do something difficult, would you not have done it? How much more, when all he said to you was, 'Wash, and be clean'?" So he went down and immersed himself seven times in the Jordan, according to the word of the man of God; his flesh was restored like the flesh of a young boy, and he was clean.

• • •

I am not a god of parlor tricks or a god who favors the rich over the poor. In fact, the important Naaman, commander of Syria's army, had to wash in a very muddy river in order to experience healing. He was initially offended by the prophet Elisha's instructions, but fortunately he followed them, and was healed. Just because I humble people does not mean I withhold healing. Remember that I am a God of love for every one of my children and wisdom for them all as well.

September 8

1 Timothy 5:1-2

• • •

Do not speak harshly to an older man, but speak to him as to a father, to younger men as brothers, to older women as mothers, to younger women as sisters—with absolute purity.

• • •

When my children recognize that you are all family to each other—across religion, across race, across culture—then perhaps you will know and create the peace I desire for you. If someone angers or frustrates you today, I invite you to engage them as family whom you seek to know and be known to. If it is hard, lift that up to me.

September 9

1 Chronicles 22:2-5

• • •

David gave orders to gather together the aliens who were residing in the land of Israel, and he set stonecutters to prepare dressed stones for building the house of God. David also provided great stores of iron for nails for the doors of the gates and for clamps, as well as bronze in quantities beyond weighing, and cedar logs without number—for the Sidonians and Tyrians brought great quantities of cedar to David. For David said, "My son Solomon is young and inexperienced, and the house that is to be built for the LORD must be exceedingly magnificent, famous and glorified throughout all lands; I will therefore make preparation for it." So David provided materials in great quantity before his death.

• • •

Some of our work spans generations. Take comfort in knowing that my son Solomon's vision of building a temple to honor me happened because his father invested in and supported him. Today I invite you to reflect on your dreams to honor me and invite someone into the role of supporting you in achieving them. You were not meant to be alone in this work.

September 10

2 Timothy 2:14b–15

• • •

...warn them before God that they are to avoid wrangling over words, which does no good but only ruins those who are listening. Do your best to present yourself to God as one approved by him, a worker who has no need to be ashamed, rightly explaining the word of truth.

• • •

Sometimes people get so hung up on presentation that they do not pay attention to what matters: content. Present yourself to me authentically and you honor me. Do not hide your questions or your pain. Do not hide your failings or your doubts. Do not use fancy words that get in the way of a conversation between us. Show up for me as your authentic self and help others do so as well, and that will please me beyond measure.

September 11

2 Chronicles 30:8-9

• • •

Do not now be stiff-necked as your ancestors were, but yield yourselves to the LORD and come to his sanctuary, which he has sanctified forever, and serve the LORD your God, so that his fierce anger may turn away from you. For as you return to the LORD, your kindred and your children will find compassion with their captors, and return to this land. For the LORD your God is gracious and merciful, and will not turn away his face from you, if you return to him."

• • •

Even after exile, my children were welcomed back by me enthusiastically. If I can welcome an entire nation as they reconciled to me, how could I not embrace you whenever you come back to me? Today I invite you to pause and reflect on the fact that no matter what you do, I will be able to welcome you when you are ready to return to me, and no matter what happens to you, I will be there to walk with you every step of the way.

September 12

Titus 3:3–5

• • •

For we ourselves were once foolish, disobedient, led astray, slaves to various passions and pleasures, passing our days in malice and envy, despicable, hating one another. But when the goodness and loving kindness of God our Savior appeared, he saved us, not because of any works of righteousness that we had done, but according to his mercy, through the water of rebirth and renewal by the Holy Spirit.

• • •

S*alvation* is a word with many meanings. Look today at what my children were saved *from*. My Son saved my children from foolishness and disobedience, lack of self-control, malice, envy, and hatred of one another. If you seek rebirth, know that my Son wants a world for you of wisdom and obedience, self-control, compassion, contentment, and love of each other. What a world that would be! And I long for you to get to live in it.

September 13

Ezra 7:27–28

• • •

Blessed be the LORD, the God of our ancestors, who put such a thing as this into the heart of the king to glorify the house of the LORD in Jerusalem, and who extended to me steadfast love before the king and his counselors, and before all the king's mighty officers. I took courage, for the hand of the LORD my God was upon me, and I gathered leaders from Israel to go up with me.

• • •

King Artaxerxes of Babylon was so moved by the testimony of my child and prophet Ezra that he sent Ezra and many of my children of Israel to Jerusalem with money for sacrifices to honor me and to investigate the possibility of healing with their siblings of Judah. When you live faithfully and speak honestly of the God of compassion and love—when you live in a way that inspires others—even the most powerful of people might take note. How might you help people with power connect to their best selves and to me as Ezra helped King Artaxerxes become enthusiastic in his support of my children?

September 14

Philemon 1:15–16

• • •

Perhaps this is the reason he was separated from you for a while, so that you might have him back forever, no longer as a slave but more than a slave, a beloved brother—especially to me but how much more to you, both in the flesh and in the Lord.

• • •

Throughout human history, people have enslaved others and rationalized or justified it, even in my name. In the Letter to Philemon, the writer reminds the reader to forgive his former slave for escaping, because now that man has returned to him an equal in my name. And this is the state I desire for all of my children, just as happened to the one written about here. Today reflect on your role in helping people escape slavery and experience new life as equals in my name.

September 15

Nehemiah 8:9-10

• • •

And Nehemiah, who was the governor, and Ezra the priest and scribe, and the Levites who taught the people said to all the people, "This day is holy to the LORD your God; do not mourn or weep." For all the people wept when they heard the words of the law. Then he said to them, "Go your way, eat the fat and drink sweet wine and send portions of them to those for whom nothing is prepared, for this day is holy to our LORD; and do not be grieved, for the joy of the LORD is your strength."

• • •

So often people think of the laws I gave my children as a burden instead of recognizing that following my laws offers freedom, because the laws of my heart protect the vulnerable and help those on the margins thrive, which leads to a glorious and healthy community. The next time you set up rules so that your community can thrive, make sure the laws follow my basic tenets of love and compassion, and if they do, then throw a party like your ancestors did!

September 16

Hebrews 6:10

• • •

For God is not unjust; he will not overlook your work and the
love that you showed for his sake in serving the saints, as you
still do.

• • •

This is all I ask of you—extend kindness to all those in
whom you encounter the divine spark...and remember
that I am in every child who walks this earth. No matter what
the world says to you, if you are caring for those in need—
those who are ignored, those who need compassion—then
I will see that and celebrate it. Your every act of kindness
brings me great joy. I see you and I honor you and I love you.

September 17

Esther 4:13b–14

• • •

"Do not think that in the king's palace you will escape any more than all the other Jews. For if you keep silence at such a time as this, relief and deliverance will rise for the Jews from another quarter, but you and your father's family will perish. Who knows? Perhaps you have come to royal dignity for just such a time as this."

• • •

My daughter Esther could have hidden and pretended not to be Jewish when her people were under attack. Her uncle Mordecai brought her this message from me, though—I would help my beloved children escape persecution even if Esther did not use her power as king's consort to help save them, but then she would not get to be part of my work of salvation. Today I invite you to reflect on how you are also Esther: who can you help because of who you know or where you work or the community whose resources you are connected to? Perhaps you are here for such a time as this.

September 18

James 2:5-7

• • •

Listen, my beloved brothers and sisters. Has not God chosen the poor in the world to be rich in faith and to be heirs of the kingdom that he has promised to those who love him? But you have dishonored the poor. Is it not the rich who oppress you? Is it not they who drag you into court? Is it not they who blaspheme the excellent name that was invoked over you?

• • •

I may never fully understand why my children, most of whom are not rich, strive to connect more deeply to the rich instead of supporting people who are poor. No matter how often my children included the teaching to care for the poor in scripture, humanity has aligned with those who mistreat them and mistreat those who are even more mistreated. If you can honor me by building relations with the poor among you, my kindom will arrive on earth so much sooner.

September 19

Job 24:2-4

• • •

The wicked remove landmarks;
    they seize flocks and pasture them.
They drive away the donkey of the orphan;
    they take the widow's ox for a pledge.
They thrust the needy off the road;
    the poor of the earth all hide themselves.

• • •

My beloved and struggling child Job spoke truly when he said that the mistreatment of those in need was a sign of true wickedness, that greed rules this world. Mistrust those who do not care for the poor—they are not in alignment with my will, and they create a world that will destroy itself. Today I invite you to reflect on the harms done to your community by people buying up and possibly tearing down historic sites, profiting off of others' needs, and displacing poor people. Pray that you might play a role in overturning their wickedness in this generation.

September 20

1 Peter 4:8–11

• • •

Above all, maintain constant love for one another, for love covers a multitude of sins. Be hospitable to one another without complaining. Like good stewards of the manifold grace of God, serve one another with whatever gift each of you has received. Whoever speaks must do so as one speaking the very words of God; whoever serves must do so with the strength that God supplies, so that God may be glorified in all things through Jesus Christ. To him belong the glory and the power forever and ever.

• • •

This scripture describes what the church on earth should look like. Love and hospitality and stewardship and service are how my Son is glorified, and a community that practices these values is how the world may know my love for them. Today ask how you can participate in strengthening these values in your community and sharing them with the world that needs them so much.

September 21

Psalms 102:25–28

• • •

Long ago you laid the foundation of the earth,
  and the heavens are the work of your hands.
They will perish, but you endure;
  they will all wear out like a garment.
You change them like clothing, and they pass away;
  but you are the same, and your years have no end.
The children of your servants shall live secure;
  their offspring shall be established in your presence.

• • •

Place your faith in me, in the eternal, and raise the next generation to do the same, because in serving me you will know a contentment that the world cannot provide. People will fail you because the sins of fear and greed abound, but I will never fail you. Place your trust in me and serve my children and you will know joy.

September 22

2 Peter 3:8–9

• • •

But do not ignore this one fact, beloved, that with the Lord one day is like a thousand years, and a thousand years are like one day. The Lord is not slow about his promise, as some think of slowness, but is patient with you, not wanting any to perish, but all to come to repentance.

• • •

People want to see my justice, or even my vengeance, thinking that I am like them. But my heart is for all of my children, and I seek for all of them to know me as a loving and compassionate God who can help them experience forgiveness and new life. My beloved child, when you get frustrated, remember that I hold the same grace and patience and love for you that I do for my other children. Know that you will never be without my love, even for one moment, far less a whole day.

September 23

Proverbs 28:1

• • •

The wicked flee when no one pursues,
    but the righteous are as bold as a lion.

• • •

It takes courage to stand by my word and my teachings. This proverb is true, but it ignores the fact that much evil in this world happens because my children stand by and permit it. Only my most faithful servants stand bold as lions for what is right. And sometimes good people are seduced by promises of more safety or more comfort so they turn a blind eye to the wickedness that buys them the illusion of safety and comfort. Today I invite you to reflect on where the world needs your boldness in standing for justice and compassion. This world needs you. Be bold for my sake, for the sake of the kindom here on earth, and for my children who suffer so others can be comfortable.

September 24

1 John 5:2–5

• • •

By this we know that we love the children of God, when we love God and obey his commandments. For the love of God is this, that we obey his commandments. And his commandments are not burdensome, for whatever is born of God conquers the world. And this is the victory that conquers the world, our faith. Who is it that conquers the world but the one who believes that Jesus is the Son of God?

• • •

What a world it will be when victors can conquer the world through obedience and faithfulness to the commands to love me and love their neighbors. Instead of victors who destroy and kill, you will know a land where victors serve and honor my teachings. This is the world I dream for you—nonviolent victory, conquering the world through love for the sake of love.

September 25

Ecclesiastes 9:13–18

• • •

I have also seen this example of wisdom under the sun, and it seemed great to me. There was a little city with few people in it. A great king came against it and besieged it, building great siegeworks against it. Now there was found in it a poor, wise man, and he by his wisdom delivered the city. Yet no one remembered that poor man. So I said, "Wisdom is better than might; yet the poor man's wisdom is despised, and his words are not heeded."

The quiet words of the wise are more to be heeded
than the shouting of a ruler among fools.
Wisdom is better than weapons of war,
but one bungler destroys much good.

• • •

This world is so often seduced by loud and aggressive voices, but the world is saved by calm and patient wisdom. Today I invite you to look for the humble but wise people in your midst and listen to them. Let their quiet words drown out the shouting of a ruler, so that you may be served by wisdom and escape the cruel weapons of war and so you may save your people from the bungler who destroys a nation or even the world.

September 26

James 5:4-5

• • •

Listen! The wages of the laborers who mowed your fields, which you kept back by fraud, cry out, and the cries of the harvesters have reached the ears of the Lord of hosts. You have lived on the earth in luxury and in pleasure; you have fattened your hearts in a day of slaughter.

• • •

Eighteen hundred years ago, some of my followers wanted to remove the book of James from the Bible because it was "too Jewish." Those followers overlooked the faithful commitment of my Jewish children to the teaching that no one is truly my follower who exploits their workers for their own gain. Today's church should be glad that some fought to keep this important letter in the Bible, because its teachings reflect the best of Judaism and the best of the Christian church: stand with the poor and you stand with me. Bring harm to the poor and you turn your back on me.

September 27

Song of Solomon 2:10-12

• • •

My beloved speaks and says to me:
"Arise, my love, my fair one,
    and come away;
for now the winter is past,
    the rain is over and gone.
The flowers appear on the earth;
    the time of singing has come,
and the voice of the turtledove
    is heard in our land."

• • •

I want for you the love that my children in this book had for each other. I want you to experience the world as they experienced it, through the eyes of love. That love may be romantic, as theirs was, or it may be the deep love of friendship. I want you to know that you are valued and treasured and loved. I also want you to learn this firsthand from my other children, and in those moments that you do not feel it from them, know that I love you and want you to know the time of singing that the writer of this scripture announces joyfully.

September 28

John 20:18

• • •

Mary Magdalene went and announced to the disciples, "I have seen the Lord"; and she told them that he had said these things to her.

• • •

You may already know that the first evangelist of my Son's resurrection was a woman. This was not a mistake on my part. My beloved daughter Mary Magdalene went on to tell the story of my love to many people, and her story has been misshapen over the years. My beloved daughter knew that some people would not believe her. She knew that many were not ready for this good news and were not ready for the good news to come from her. She did not let that stop her. What news of my love will you share today, even if people are not ready to hear it?

September 29

Isaiah 54:13–14

• • •

All your children shall be taught by the LORD,
    and great shall be the prosperity of your children.
In righteousness you shall be established;
    you shall be far from oppression, for you shall not fear;
    and from terror, for it shall not come near you.

• • •

My beloved children had suffered much by the time they heard this word from my prophet. Good news for them was that their children would know me and learn from me, that I would stay with the generations after theirs, and that they would not need to live in fear any longer. Today I invite you to think about the well-being of the next generation, and to pray for how they may be freed from the sins of your generation, so that you may know peace and comfort.

September 30

John 20:27-29

• • •

Then he said to Thomas, "Put your finger here and see my hands. Reach out your hand and put it in my side. Do not doubt but believe." Thomas answered him, "My Lord and my God!" Jesus said to him, "Have you believed because you have seen me? Blessed are those who have not seen and yet have come to believe."

• • •

Often people read this as a story of judgment on "Doubting Thomas." But my Son offered the proof that his beloved brother Thomas asked for, because he knew how hurt Thomas was at losing someone he loved so much. But my Son also knew how much more he was asking of you, that you believe even when he is not standing there with you in physical form. So today I ask you to close your eyes and imagine your brother Jesus with an arm of comfort around you, encouraging you and showing you support and love. You deserve to know the love of your brother Jesus.

October

365 LOVE NOTES FROM GOD

October 1

Jeremiah 30:17

For I will restore health to you,
    and your wounds I will heal,
        says the LORD,
because they have called you an outcast:
    "It is Zion; no one cares for her!"

Think of a neighborhood or city or state or country that people have given up on. Now ask yourself, do any of my children live there? Finally, ask yourself if I care about those people. In the same way that I never gave up on my children of Zion, I have not given up on that place. Today I invite you to pray for healing and health for the people of that neighborhood or city or state or country, and I invite you to find out how you might support them in some way so they are reminded that I have not forgotten them.

October 2

Revelation 22:5

• • •

And there will be no more night; they need no light of lamp or sun, for the Lord God will be their light, and they will reign forever and ever.

• • •

So many people have misused the Book of Revelation to promote false teachings about my role in saving some people and condemning others to great horrors. But it was intended to help the church survive an oppressive empire and draw hope from knowing that evil would not prevail, even though they were suffering. It reminded them that ultimately what waited for them was rest and comfort and healing and thriving in my arms. Likewise, beloved, know that while I call you to resist empires that cause the poor to suffer, and while that may not be an easy path, what waits for you is rest and comfort and healing and thriving in my arms. Be brave, my beloved child. The world needs you, and I am with you.

October 3

Lamentations 3:25–28,31–33

• • •

The LORD is good to those who wait for him,
    to the soul that seeks him.
It is good that one should wait quietly
    for the salvation of the LORD.
It is good for one to bear
    the yoke in youth,
to sit alone in silence
    when the Lord has imposed it,...
For the Lord will not
    reject forever.
Although he causes grief, he will have compassion
    according to the abundance of his steadfast love;
for he does not willingly afflict
    or grieve anyone.

• • •

In this world of frenzy and rush and pressure to produce, when is the last time that you sat alone in silence? Give yourself that gift today. If the silence surfaces your grief, let me hold it with you. If that silence makes you confront the ways you feel rejected, let me hold you. Know that I am in the silence, and I am both in and with you.

October 4

Matthew 5:23-24

• • •

So when you are offering your gift at the altar, if you remember that your brother or sister has something against you, leave your gift there before the altar and go; first be reconciled to your brother or sister, and then come and offer your gift.

• • •

My Son was reminding you, and the generations before and after you, that an offering to me is of little value if it comes amidst conflict and hostility. When you right the wrongs you have created, when you restore relations with someone you have harmed, that in and of itself is the offering I desire, and then I will be able to celebrate your gift to me. Know that this can be a lifelong journey. Know that I am with you at whatever step you are in that process, and I will keep carrying you forward.

October 5

Ezekiel 37:1–3a

• • •

The hand of the LORD came upon me, and he brought me out by the spirit of the LORD and set me down in the middle of a valley; it was full of bones. He led me all round them; there were very many lying in the valley, and they were very dry. He said to me, "Mortal, can these bones live?"

• • •

Poor Ezekiel. He could sense that I was asking him a trick question. He said to me that only I could know the answer, which was true, although he answered this way to avoid being wrong. And yet, he was wise when he said that anything was possible with me. What part of your life feels like these dry bones? What part of your community? Lift those up to me in prayer, that I might breathe life into them, and that you might testify to the fact that they can live again.

October 6

Mark 9:35

• • •

He sat down, called the twelve, and said to them, "Whoever wants to be first must be last of all and servant of all."

• • •

What the world rewards and what I reward are so different. Imagine a community that places the most humble servant in the position of decision maker. Instead of a world where certain people are expected to be servants and others expected to lead, imagine a community where everyone understands themselves as servants of each other. That is the community I want you to create, to maintain, to teach about so that once built, the community is constantly reminded that all are to be servants of each other. Imagine what it will feel like for your community to take care of your needs because they know they need to serve you as you serve them.

October 7

Daniel 9:18–19

• • •

"Incline your ear, O my God, and hear. Open your eyes and look at our desolation and the city that bears your name. We do not present our supplication before you on the ground of our righteousness, but on the ground of your great mercies. O Lord, hear; O Lord, forgive; O Lord, listen and act and do not delay! For your own sake, O my God, because your city and your people bear your name!"

• • •

How many people in your city are lifting up this kind of prayer to me? And what do those prayers seek? I listen for prayers seeking healing, seeking redemption, seeking a new way of being community in the days to come. I listen for prayers that are humble and confess the limitations of a people. One of my beloved servants once said, "You pray for the poor. Then you feed the poor. That is how prayer works." Are your people praying the prayers that my son Daniel prayed for his people and then living out those prayers? If not, what might your community look like if they did?

October 8

Luke 7:33–35

• • •

"For John the Baptist has come eating no bread and drinking no wine, and you say, 'He has a demon'; the Son of Man has come eating and drinking, and you say, 'Look, a glutton and a drunkard, a friend of tax collectors and sinners!' Nevertheless, wisdom is vindicated by all her children."

• • •

My children can be petty and jealous and self-righteous. If that is ever directed at you, listen to the true and comforting words my Son offered: wisdom is vindicated by all her children. In other words, your actions in the world will speak powerfully enough to drown out the petty people undermining you. Stay faithful to my teachings and do my work, and you will be lifted up on the wings of the Holy Spirit, no matter who tries to tear you down.

October 9

Hosea 10:13–14a

• • •

You have ploughed wickedness,
    you have reaped injustice,
    you have eaten the fruit of lies.
Because you have trusted in your power
    and in the multitude of your warriors,
therefore the tumult of war shall rise against your people,
    and all your fortresses shall be destroyed

• • •

The tragedy of war is that it decimates the loser, but it also destroys the winner in many ways. My way is not "might makes right," and yet my children fall prey to that path over and over. Whenever your nation trusts in its leaders more than in me, or whenever your country believes I have endorsed violence, know that even if you win, you do not win. Today pray to trust me more than a multitude of warriors, for the healing of your land.

October 10

John 12:35–36

• • •

Jesus said to them, "The light is with you for a little longer. Walk while you have the light, so that the darkness may not overtake you. If you walk in the darkness, you do not know where you are going. While you have the light, believe in the light, so that you may become children of light."

• • •

What would it look like to walk through the world as if the light of my Son were guiding you? What might you see that isn't visible right now? What paths might you follow if that light were cast, instead of the path seeming shadowy and scary? I want that life for you—a life illuminated with my love—so that you can go boldly in the path I have set for you, unafraid of the dark.

October 11

Joel 3:14

• • •

Multitudes, multitudes,
    in the valley of decision!
For the day of the LORD is near
    in the valley of decision.

• • •

My son Joel renamed the Valley of Jehoshaphat ("Yahweh judges") the "valley of decision" (or sharp valley, cut valley, or diligent valley depending on who translates the Hebrew). Where others saw it as the place where I would destroy the nations and punish Zion's enemies, this translation invites you to consider what it means to *choose* what you will do and how you will be judged. What decision will you make today, among the multitudes ignoring the power to choose and following the crowd?

October 12

Acts 10:25–28

• • •

On Peter's arrival Cornelius met him, and falling at his feet, worshiped him. But Peter made him get up, saying, "Stand up; I am only a mortal." And as he talked with him, he went in and found that many had assembled; and he said to them, "You yourselves know that it is unlawful for a Jew to associate with or to visit a Gentile; but God has shown me that I should not call anyone profane or unclean.

• • •

My law is in place to keep people in line with my will. My will is for healing and wholeness and connection between all of my children. Which law is creating barriers between you and me? Which law is creating barriers between you and healthy connections with others of my children? Pray that my law of love might guide you to the path I desire for you and your community.

October 13

Amos 5:23–24

• • •

Take away from me the noise of your songs;
    I will not listen to the melody of your harps.
But let justice roll down like waters,
    and righteousness like an ever-flowing stream.

• • •

This is a popular and much romanticized passage, but my son Amos was so outraged on my behalf at the lack of justice, at the corruption and the mistreatment of the poor, that he called for a torrential flood. People who lived there at the time lived on a flood plain and knew what the costs of justice rolling down like waters could be. So did Amos. Today I invite you to reflect on the thing in your community that needs to be cleansed, and the corruption or mistreatment of people in need. I invite you to feel my outrage at that injustice so deeply that you feel the same righteous outrage as my son Amos. Then think about how to channel that outrage in a way that honors me.

October 14

Romans 8:22-25

• • •

We know that the whole creation has been groaning in labor pains until now; and not only the creation, but we ourselves, who have the first fruits of the Spirit, groan inwardly while we wait for adoption, the redemption of our bodies. For in hope we were saved. Now hope that is seen is not hope. For who hopes for what is seen? But if we hope for what we do not see, we wait for it with patience.

• • •

My precious children in the church of Rome chose to follow my Son because they were promised he would return. They even believed he would return in their lifetime. My beloved son Paul (who also believed he would see Jesus' return, even though he hadn't met him before my Son's crucifixion) wrote these words to comfort and encourage his flock. Today I invite you to reflect on something you hope for that this world may never see, and I ask you to hope for it anyhow. Hope is how generations of faithful Christians have created glimpses of my kindom on earth. Hope followed by action is one of the most faithful acts in the face of a world that tells you something worth hoping for can never happen.

October 15

Obadiah 1:15

• • •

For the day of the LORD is near against all the nations.
As you have done, it shall be done to you;
   your deeds shall return on your own head.

• • •

Sometimes my children today wish I would punish the unjust more than I do. Some of my children imagine that when something bad happens, it is the result of my punishing power. When you hear someone misrepresent me by saying I destroyed a city with a hurricane because that city accepts my teaching that love is love, remind them of this passage, where my son Obadiah pointed out that evil actions rebound on the actor. I do not need to punish my children: you punish yourselves when you act selfishly or unjustly.

October 16

1 Corinthians 11:20-22a

• • •

When you come together, it is not really to eat the Lord's supper. For when the time comes to eat, each of you goes ahead with your own supper, and one goes hungry and another becomes drunk. What! Do you not have homes to eat and drink in? Or do you show contempt for the church of God and humiliate those who have nothing?

• • •

In the first days, communion was a full meal that my children shared in common to honor my Son's life, death, and resurrection. It also served to make sure those in need had enough to eat. Fairly soon, though, my son Paul had to adjust communion to make it a symbolic meal because those with power and resources did not distribute the communion meal fairly so that all who had need would be fed physically as well as spiritually. What religious acts today do not honor my call to treat all people equally? What might need to change to better honor me and those in need?

October 17

Jonah 4:10b–11

• • •

"You are concerned about the bush, for which you did not labor and which you did not grow; it came into being in a night and perished in a night. And should I not be concerned about Nineveh, that great city, in which there are more than a hundred and twenty thousand people who do not know their right hand from their left, and also many animals?"

• • •

My poor and faithful son Jonah did what he was told (eventually) even though he did not want to. And when he sat under a bush and I killed it, he was grieved to the point of wanting to die. I reminded him that the people from Nineveh, the land he hated, were also valuable, even more perhaps than a shrub. What land do you or does your nation hate? Today think about the majority of people in that land who do not want to participate in hate or do not want war or do not want harm to come to you or do not know any better than to also hate your nation. Reflect on their lives and what they mean to me, and pray for them.

October 18

2 Corinthians 9:6-7

• • •

The point is this: the one who sows sparingly will also reap sparingly, and the one who sows bountifully will also reap bountifully. Each of you must give as you have made up your mind, not reluctantly or under compulsion, for God loves a cheerful giver.

• • •

This is some of the most practical advice ever given by one of my children: people are not prone to being generous to someone who is stingy. Even the land does not offer up its best to someone who does not tend it well and seed it abundantly. People often use this quote to encourage giving to the collection plate, as if I mean I want the money for myself and it is how you honor me. What this passage really means is that you should treat your siblings, my children, with generosity. Today reflect on what could help you be a cheerful giver to your fellow human beings.

October 19

Micah 6:7–8

• • •

"Will the Lord be pleased with thousands of rams,
    with ten thousands of rivers of oil?
Shall I give my firstborn for my transgression,
    the fruit of my body for the sin of my soul?"
He has told you, O mortal, what is good;
    and what does the Lord require of you
but to do justice, and to love kindness,
    and to walk humbly with your God?

• • •

You are an offering. I don't need stuff. I don't need rams or oil or buildings as an act to honor me or to seek my forgiveness. Some of my children have said that humanity's problem is that you love justice and do kindness instead of what Micah told you to do. So today I invite you to think about an act you can engage in to create systems of justice for many people, and find one small way of acting on that.

October 20

Galatians 5:1

• • •

For freedom Christ has set us free. Stand firm, therefore, and do not submit again to a yoke of slavery.

• • •

My son Paul meant this passage to encourage a church that frustrated him to urge them to stand more boldly for what they believed instead of getting seduced by the pagan practices around them or the old Jewish codes they were using to shut out new believers in Christ who weren't Jewish. But today I invite you to reflect on the passage more broadly. Reflect on what holds you back, enslaving you to customs and traditions and practices you know are wrong. Pray to me for the courage to stand firm and experience true freedom in standing with me for justice and liberation for all my children.

October 21

Nahum 3:19

• • •

There is no assuaging your hurt,
   your wound is mortal.
All who hear the news about you
   clap their hands over you.
For who has ever escaped
   your endless cruelty?

• • •

My son Nahum was warning the people of Nineveh that they had behaved in such ugly fashion that people would rejoice when I brought that place down. All cities that revert to cruelty do end up bringing themselves low. Today I invite you to pray for your city, that its heart might be softened and turned to compassion, that its residents might know love and gentleness amidst the hard realities of their lives. Pray that you might have a role in making your community less like Nineveh and more like Eden.

October 22

Ephesians 4:25–27

• • •

So then, putting away falsehood, let all of us speak the truth to our neighbors, for we are members of one another. Be angry but do not sin; do not let the sun go down on your anger, and do not make room for the devil.

• • •

Often this advice is given to couples getting married so that they resolve conflicts as they arise rather than holding onto their hurts overnight. Place it in its context, though: my Son's earliest followers came from different classes and genders and regions and were trying to build a life together across many cultural differences, in ways that transgressed the values of patriarchy and tribalism. This is my child's advice to a new, fragile community seeking to be faithful to me even though they had so little in common. Patriarchy and tribalism are still widespread, and people do not live together across cultural differences. How might you play a role in building a church like the one in Ephesus, and then make sure that the incredibly diverse group found ways to work and live and love and worship together? Cast that vision with me today so that I can help you live into it in the days to come.

296

October 23

Habakkuk 2:4-5

• • •

Look at the proud!
　　Their spirit is not right in them,
　　but the righteous live by their faith.
Moreover, wealth is treacherous;
　　the arrogant do not endure.
They open their throats wide as Sheol;
　　like Death they never have enough.
They gather all nations for themselves,
　　and collect all peoples as their own.

• • •

A famous billionaire in the United States was interviewed in the 1980s about his wealth. "Do you consider yourself rich?" he was asked. He said no. When asked how much it would take for him to feel rich, he said, "just another $20 million." From the beginning of time greed has been a bottomless void for those trapped by it. Today pray that you will be protected from a greed that leads people to harm others and still brings no real and lasting joy.

October 24

Philippians 3:18–20

• • •

For many live as enemies of the cross of Christ; I have often told you of them, and now I tell you even with tears. Their end is destruction; their god is the belly; and their glory is in their shame; their minds are set on earthly things. But our citizenship is in heaven, and it is from there that we are expecting a Savior, the Lord Jesus Christ.

• • •

My children who are the most free are the ones who do not long for earthly treasures. I know how hard that is: advertising tells you that you need to buy things and dress certain ways and eat certain foods to know happiness. Those things do not bring joy, but they trap people in the pursuit of a joy they will never achieve. Today I invite you to practice rejecting the world's seductions and turn instead to building my Realm on earth, where you can know my love and the love of my Son.

October 25

Zephaniah 3:1-2

• • •

Ah, soiled, defiled,
 oppressing city!
It has listened to no voice;
 it has accepted no correction.
It has not trusted in the LORD;
 it has not drawn near to its God.

• • •

Every empire that oppressed and exploited has fallen. Sometimes it has fallen to other oppressing and exploiting empires, and sometimes it has fallen under its own weight. Disregard for my most oppressed children weakens a city or state or nation, because it distances that place from me. Today pray for your community that it might create equity for all of my children and therefore grow close to me once again.

October 26

Colossians 3:8-11

• • •

But now you must get rid of all such things—anger, wrath, malice, slander, and abusive language from your mouth. Do not lie to one another, seeing that you have stripped off the old self with its practices and have clothed yourselves with the new self, which is being renewed in knowledge according to the image of its creator. In that renewal there is no longer Greek and Jew, circumcised and uncircumcised, barbarian, Scythian, slave and free; but Christ is all and in all!

• • •

In every generation, humanity's fear drives you to create "us and them." Sometimes a minority group is trying to protect itself, but it often tries to protect itself from the wrong people. This early church had many divisions that stopped them from joining together to recognize their shared suffering under the Roman empire that hated me and punished them for loving me. My beloved child who wrote this letter pleaded with them to remember their allegiance to Jesus Christ amidst their many conflicts and differences, so they could create a community who resisted Rome's teachings that Caesar was a god, instead uniting around the subversive idea that only I was God, which meant Caesar was only a man. Today I invite you to reflect on who you have been divided from, so that you may be united with them in Christ to subvert the oppressive empire that exists today to harm many with impunity.

October 27

Haggai 2:18b–19

• • •

Since the day that the foundation of the LORD's temple was laid, consider: Is there any seed left in the barn? Do the vine, the fig tree, the pomegranate, and the olive tree still yield nothing? From this day on I will bless you.

• • •

My child who wrote this text longed for my children to worship me. Rebuilding the temple helped his people remember who they were, reorienting themselves toward my lifesaving laws that would help them once again be a community of compassion and care and ethics and values that had been lost in exile. What thrives in your faith community when you worship me and follow my laws of compassion and care and ethics and values?

October 28

1 Thessalonians 5:12–13

• • •

But we appeal to you, brothers and sisters, to respect those who labor among you, and have charge of you in the Lord and admonish you; esteem them very highly in love because of their work. Be at peace among yourselves.

• • •

So many of the letters in the early church were about resolving conflict, creating structures, dismantling preexisting hierarchies and sometimes creating new ones. Not everyone loved giving up power and following the guidance and wisdom of new authority. How many of the new converts from merchant cities, people of wealth, would normally have signed up to be led by a bunch of fishermen from an outlying region of little importance? My path often upsets existing power structures. This can create tension, but my faithful children can work through it. Today reflect on where power structures need to change, who will be affected, and how finding unity in my Son might help people move into a new way of being.

October 29

Zechariah 12:10

• • •

And I will pour out a spirit of compassion and supplication on the house of David and the inhabitants of Jerusalem, so that, when they look on the one whom they have pierced, they shall mourn for him, as one mourns for an only child, and weep bitterly over him, as one weeps over a firstborn.

• • •

My child who wrote this passage did not think that his current time held much promise, but he knew I would come to create healing for his people. He knew his people would do harm to the best of their own, but through their relationship with me they would come to understand their sin, repent, and be reunited with me. Who is it that your society has pierced, whether it be innocents in war abroad or in a militarized state at home? Pray that your society will mourn for them as one mourns for an only child, as the first step in being reconciled to me.

October 30

2 Thessalonians 3:13

• • •

Brothers and sisters, do not be weary in doing what is right.

• • •

This passage may seem simple or obvious or inspirational in a way that makes you want to put it on a coffee mug. My child who wrote it knew that it can be wearying to follow me because there is so much resistance. So the writer offered these words to his family of choice as a comfort— he knew they *were* tired, and he reminded them of the dignity and the sacred in what they were doing. Likewise, my beloved child, I see the dignity and the sacred in you doing what is right even when that requires a sacrifice, even when ignoring justice for the poor or ignoring oppression would make your life easier. Know that I am shouldering the burden with you, and may this knowledge ease your burden.

October 31

Malachi 4:5–6

• • •

Lo, I will send you the prophet Elijah before the great and terrible day of the LORD comes. He will turn the hearts of parents to their children and the hearts of children to their parents, so that I will not come and strike the land with a curse.

• • •

When the generations heal the conflict between them, when you and your parents and grandparents, and your children and grandchildren all seek each other's thriving, that will be my Realm on Earth. Some of my children called Native Americans say that every action should be for the well-being of the seventh generation after this one. That is the world I want for you—where everything you and your community and your nation and this world do is for the seventh generation after yours.

November 1

Genesis 39:23

• • •

The chief jailer paid no heed to anything that was in Joseph's care, because the LORD was with him; and whatever he did, the LORD made it prosper.

• • •

There is a reason my Son told his followers that part of how he knew they were good was that "when I was in prison, you visited me." Like today, prison in Joseph's time was an awful place. And yet Joseph's faithfulness to me, and his willingness to follow my ways, meant he had a path to surviving that awful place. Remember that my love and care can creep into even the harshest places and the narrowest crevices, into jail cells of ancient times and jail cells of today...and into the places in your heart that do not yet believe you deserve the love I offer.

November 2

1 Timothy 6:11-12

• • •

But as for you, man of God, shun all this; pursue righteousness, godliness, faith, love, endurance, gentleness. Fight the good fight of the faith; take hold of the eternal life, to which you were called and for which you made the good confession in the presence of many witnesses.

• • •

Beloved child, today I invite you to reflect on what it will look like for you to fight the good fight of the faith. Then I want you to consider the weapons I am giving you for this fight: righteousness, godliness, faith, love, endurance, and gentleness. Which of those weapons do you need to hone, and how will you use them in this nonviolent fight I am inviting you to join?

November 3

Exodus 40:36–38

• • •

Whenever the cloud was taken up from the tabernacle, the Israelites would set out on each stage of their journey; but if the cloud was not taken up, then they did not set out until the day that it was taken up. For the cloud of the LORD was on the tabernacle by day, and fire was in the cloud by night, before the eyes of all the house of Israel at each stage of their journey.

• • •

Throughout all of time I have set out signs for my children to follow. Following the cloud kept my beloved children alive as they wandered the desert and recovered from the trauma of slavery in Egypt. None of them had known freedom, and it would have been overwhelming without signs that I was there to guide them. I offer you signs, also, of the life I am calling you into. Today reflect on what signs, like the cloud that led the Israelites, are waiting to help you follow your life's calling.

November 4

2 Timothy 2:16

• • •

Avoid profane chatter, for it will lead people into more and more impiety.

• • •

You may have noticed by now how many of my children writing to the early church talked about the dangers of gossip. In that new and fragile community, gossip could destroy a burgeoning movement. In your faith community, gossip can destroy people's trust in my followers in lasting ways. How might you help your community represent me better in the world through using only kind and direct speech, and avoiding gossip?

November 5

Leviticus 22:20

• • •

You shall not offer anything that has a blemish, for it will not be acceptable in your behalf.

• • •

I do not ask for your best offerings because I am vain. I ask for your best offerings because in striving for excellence, you may find yourself. I ask for your best offerings because what you offer to me should then be offered to those in need, because they hold my divine spark. And yet the world ignores them, and me. How might you offer me your best, and thereby heal the world?

November 6

Titus 3:6-7

• • •

This Spirit he poured out on us richly through Jesus Christ our Savior, so that, having been justified by his grace, we might become heirs according to the hope of eternal life.

• • •

When people become heirs of financial wealth, when they inherit money, they may selfishly hoard it for themselves and their immediate family, or they may share it generously, knowing an inheritance is about their good luck and not their hard work. Today, my beloved child, I want to invite you to reflect on what it means to inherit the riches of grace and to inherit access to the Holy Spirit, which is also a result of my generosity and not your hard work. Will you hoard these gifts or share them? What will that look like?

November 7

Numbers 30:1-2

• • •

Then Moses said to the heads of the tribes of the Israelites: This is what the LORD has commanded. When a man makes a vow to the LORD, or swears an oath to bind himself by a pledge, he shall not break his word; he shall do according to all that proceeds out of his mouth.

• • •

When you make a commitment to me, I take that commitment seriously. Another of my children said, "do not swear but let your yes be your yes and your no be your no." He meant that you should engage in fulfilling your promises in a humble way rather than be grandiose. In other words, honor your word; mean what you say. Today I invite you to consider what it means to be brave enough to make a promise to me and humble enough to do so quietly and simply.

November 8

Philemon 1:17–18

• • •

So if you consider me your partner, welcome him as you would welcome me. If he has wronged you in any way, or owes you anything, charge that to my account.

• • •

My child who wrote this letter modeled what it means to vouch for someone who might not be well received on their own. Because he believed in his new apostle, he staked his own resources on backing up that man. Who in your world could do their work better if you encouraged, mentored, and supported them and also lent them your credibility? Your voice matters and makes a difference.

November 9

Deuteronomy 4:39

• • •

So acknowledge today and take to heart that the Lord is God in heaven above and on the earth beneath; there is no other.

• • •

What would it be like to relate to the earth as if I were walking it alongside you? How might you and all people connect with the land as sacred? Would people buy and sell it, would they still extract oil from it in the same ways? Would we encourage more connection with it? Your ancestors knew that I am on the earth as well as in heaven. I invite you today to notice where I'm showing up on the soil beneath your feet. I invite you to connect with me there.

November 10

Hebrews 13:1-3

• • •

Let mutual love continue. Do not neglect to show hospitality to strangers, for by doing that some have entertained angels without knowing it. Remember those who are in prison, as though you were in prison with them; those who are being tortured, as though you yourselves were being tortured.

• • •

In the earliest days of the church, people had to learn to show compassion to strangers because those strangers might become part of their small but quickly growing family. They had to learn to overcome their bias against prisoners and people tortured by the Roman empire, because any of them might suffer the same fate for following my Son. I invite you to continue this practice—to cultivate empathy for those who are suffering, even if your instinct is to blame them for their suffering. Leave the judgment to me and focus on reflecting my love to all who need it.

November 11

Joshua 24:15

• • •

"Now if you are unwilling to serve the Lord, choose this day whom you will serve, whether the gods your ancestors served in the region beyond the River or the gods of the Amorites in whose land you are living; but as for me and my household, we will serve the Lord."

• • •

After the battle at Jericho, Joshua invited those who had witnessed miracles to choose: remain loyal to the gods of the land they had claimed, or follow me. The gods look different today, and many people say they follow me but actually worship other things, but the choice remains the same. So today I simply invite you to reflect on how you will reject the gods in whose land you are living—reflect again on what people around you invest in and put above all else—and ask yourself whether you will intentionally reject those gods and choose me.

November 12

James 2:14-18

• • •

What good is it, my brothers and sisters, if you say you have faith but do not have works? Can faith save you? If a brother or sister is naked and lacks daily food, and one of you says to them, "Go in peace; keep warm and eat your fill," and yet you do not supply their bodily needs, what is the good of that? So faith by itself, if it has no works, is dead. But someone will say, "You have faith and I have works." Show me your faith apart from your works, and I by my works will show you my faith.

• • •

This debate has raged since my Son first rose: which matters more, faith or works? My child who wrote this text showed that the two cannot be separated. Works without faith are empty and will not sustain. Faith without works completely misunderstands what it means to be in relationship with me. Today I send you forth with this blessing: may your faith in me run so deep that it causes you to share my love with those in need. That is what faith ultimately looks like.

November 13

Judges 11:39-40

• • •

At the end of two months, she returned to her father, who did with her according to the vow he had made. She had never slept with a man. So there arose an Israelite custom that for four days every year the daughters of Israel would go out to lament the daughter of Jephthah the Gileadite.

• • •

My beloved daughter had done nothing wrong; she simply got wrapped up in a bad faith bargain her father made with me. In exchange for his wish, he had promised me he would kill the first one who greeted him, assuming it would be his dog. Instead it was his loving daughter. To this day it breaks my heart that Jephthah so misunderstood me that he thought I would need him to go through with that sacrifice, especially after I had showed I do not want harm to come to my children when Abraham thought he should sacrifice his son Isaac to me. My beloved child, may you never misunderstand my love in such a tragic way. I never wish harm to befall my children. And I wish no harm to befall you.

November 14

1 Peter 5:6-9

• • •

Humble yourselves therefore under the mighty hand of God, so that he may exalt you in due time. Cast all your anxiety on him, because he cares for you. Discipline yourselves; keep alert. Like a roaring lion your adversary the devil prowls around, looking for someone to devour. Resist him, steadfast in your faith, for you know that your brothers and sisters in all the world are undergoing the same kinds of suffering.

• • •

Life in this world is hard. Evil is real. When the stress of it is too much, know that you can hand it over to me. And know that you are not alone—people around the world are working to make this place better. Some of them are doing it at great risk to themselves. When you follow my path, you will always have me with you, and you are also connected to everyone dedicating themselves to building my Realm on earth.

November 15

Ruth 4:14–15

• • •

Then the women said to Naomi, "Blessed be the LORD, who has not left you this day without next-of-kin; and may his name be renowned in Israel! He shall be to you a restorer of life and a nourisher of your old age; for your daughter-in-law who loves you, who is more to you than seven sons, has borne him."

• • •

Ruth and Naomi had faced so much together across two different cultures. They were closer than any couple could be. They strategized in order to survive in a world where widows had few options, and their legacy lives on to this day. At the time this book was written, Jewish people did not trust outsiders. The Book of Ruth exists as a reminder to every generation that I welcome people of all tribes and nations, and that any person from any place may be one of my greatest leaders. Who is the Ruth in your community? How will you make sure she is made welcome?

November 16

2 Peter 3:13–15a

• • •

But, in accordance with his promise, we wait for new heavens and a new earth, where righteousness is at home. Therefore, beloved, while you are waiting for these things, strive to be found by him at peace, without spot or blemish; and regard the patience of our Lord as salvation.

• • •

Two thousand years ago your ancestors waited for my Son's return. Two thousand years later many still wait. My Son made it clear that you would never know the day nor the hour of his return, and should focus instead on building the new heaven and earth today. Because in between my Son's resurrection and his return, you are Christ in the world; your faith community is Christ in the world. The way people will know that a new heaven and earth are possible is through your actions. Today I invite you to make waiting into an action rather than a passive thing, for the sake of my children in your midst.

November 17

1 Samuel 12:19-21

• • •

All the people said to Samuel, "Pray to the LORD your God for your servants, so that we may not die; for we have added to all our sins the evil of demanding a king for ourselves." And Samuel said to the people, "Do not be afraid; you have done all this evil, yet do not turn aside from following the LORD, but serve the LORD with all your heart; and do not turn aside after useless things that cannot profit or save, for they are useless.

• • •

My faithful son Samuel listened to my children when they realized that a king would not bring them what they wanted, any more than judges had done. Samuel had warned them this was true, that the only ruler they needed was me, and yet he did my will when he told them that their demand for a king need not get in the way of their relationship with me. No matter the political order in place, you and your community can always connect or reconnect or stay connected with me...even if you put that political order in place yourselves. Nothing can come between us.

November 18

1 John 5:20

• • •

And we know that the Son of God has come and has given us understanding so that we may know him who is true; and we are in him who is true, in his Son Jesus Christ. He is the true God and eternal life.

• • •

Understanding comes in many forms, from academic study to learning by experience. My beloved child wrote about the understanding that my Holy Spirit bestows in all her wisdom; it is the understanding of the heart. This understanding can help you recognize that you are part of something much greater than yourself, since you are in my Son Jesus just as he is in you, just as I am in you. Today I invite you to reflect on how you, my beloved child, are connected to all of the universe from its beginning to its end, through the Holy Spirit that dwells in you.

November 19

2 Samuel 12:5-7;9a

• • •

Then David's anger was greatly kindled against the man. He said to Nathan, "As the LORD lives, the man who has done this deserves to die; he shall restore the lamb fourfold, because he did this thing, and because he had no pity." Nathan said to David, "You are the man! Thus says the LORD, the God of Israel: I anointed you king over Israel, and I rescued you from the hand of Saul… Why have you despised the word of the LORD, to do what is evil in his sight?"

• • •

Nathan was David's best friend, closer to him than even a spouse could be. And part of that deep intimacy meant that Nathan could tell David a story of a great injustice, David could become outraged at this injustice, and then his beloved Nathan could say, "You are the man in the story I just told. You have acted against the God who supported you all your life." David had acted out of greed and selfishness and had turned to violence to get what he wanted. And his friend had the courage to tell him he was wrong. Today I invite you to pray that you have someone in your life to tell you when you have fallen away from me, someone to whom you will listen.

November 20

James 5:7-8

• • •

Be patient, therefore, beloved, until the coming of the Lord. The farmer waits for the precious crop from the earth, being patient with it until it receives the early and the late rains. You also must be patient. Strengthen your hearts, for the coming of the Lord is near.

• • •

Today I invite you to reflect on the relationships you are tending with people in need. Your life of service to me is a field to be sowed and tended. As one of my children once said, "We tend the fields whose crops we will not see." How are you tilling the soil to make sure that those in need are well-tended and can be nurtured to flourishing?

November 21

1 Kings 19:11b–13

• • •

Now there was a great wind, so strong that it was splitting mountains and breaking rocks in pieces before the Lord, but the Lord was not in the wind; and after the wind an earthquake, but the Lord was not in the earthquake; and after the earthquake a fire, but the Lord was not in the fire; and after the fire a sound of sheer silence. When Elijah heard it, he wrapped his face in his mantle and went out and stood at the entrance of the cave. Then there came a voice to him that said, "What are you doing here, Elijah?"

• • •

People often come to me seeking a circus act, a big and flashy show. How in tune with me was my child Elijah that he knew to seek me in the silence. When he stood in the silence, humbly, and waited for me, he heard me. Today I invite you to practice the discipline of listening for me in the silences. This world is so loud it seeks to drown me out. What might I whisper to you in intentional silences?

November 22

John 21:15

• • •

Jesus said to Simon Peter, "Simon son of John, do you love me more than these?" He said to him, "Yes, Lord; you know that I love you." Jesus said to him, "Feed my lambs."

• • •

When my Son returned after his resurrection and spent time with his beloved brother Peter, Peter was a little cautious with his feelings. Jesus said, "Do you love me with a sacred and binding love?" And Peter responded, "Jesus, you know I love you like a brother." Jesus understood Peter's heart was fragile still after the trauma he had gone through, so Jesus told Peter instead what truly loving him would look like: to take care of all the people Jesus loved. The same is true for you. I will know your love by how you care for my children. And I want you to receive the same care in your community.

November 23

2 Kings 12:13–14

• • •

But for the house of the LORD no basins of silver, snuffers, bowls, trumpets, or any vessels of gold, or of silver, were made from the money that was brought into the house of the LORD, for that was given to the workers who were repairing the house of the LORD with it.

• • •

From the earliest of days my children knew that once money has been made sacred, its best use is to care for the workers, the poor, the people who are most likely to be ignored by those in power. In the earliest days, those who built a temple in tribute to me knew that the best tribute to me was treating the workers building the temple with dignity. How might your faith community follow this ancient teaching?

November 24

John 21:20–22

• • •

Peter turned and saw the disciple whom Jesus loved following them; he was the one who had reclined next to Jesus at the supper and had said, "Lord, who is it that is going to betray you?" When Peter saw him, he said to Jesus, "Lord, what about him?" Jesus said to him, "If it is my will that he remain until I come, what is that to you? Follow me!"

• • •

Very often, my children think they know better than I who is worthy to be part of my flock. When the disciple whom my Son loved fled from him while he was on the cross, perhaps my child Peter thought this disciple was no longer worthy to remain in my Son's movement. Perhaps Peter forgot that if his own denial of Jesus could be forgiven, so could any disciple's shortcoming. But Jesus remembered, and so do I. Despite any of your shortcomings, I have a ministry for you. And when you question someone else being part of this movement, remember that I have a role for them too.

November 25

1 Chronicles 29:14–18

• • •

"But who am I, and what is my people, that we should be able to make this freewill offering? For all things come from you, and of your own have we given you. For we are aliens and transients before you, as were all our ancestors; our days on the earth are like a shadow, and there is no hope. O Lᴏʀᴅ our God, all this abundance that we have provided for building you a house for your holy name comes from your hand and is all your own. I know, my God, that you search the heart, and take pleasure in uprightness; in the uprightness of my heart I have freely offered all these things, and now I have seen your people, who are present here, offering freely and joyously to you. O Lᴏʀᴅ, the God of Abraham, Isaac, and Israel, our ancestors, keep forever such purposes and thoughts in the hearts of your people, and direct their hearts toward you."

• • •

Think about what this prayer means to you and your community and your nation today. What would it look like for your community to treat all things as if they belong to me instead of as if they are commodities that can be owned by you? What does it mean to think of yourselves as foreigners and people without a home? What does it mean to claim Abraham, Isaac, and Israel as your ancestors? Today I invite you to read this prayer out loud as if it is about you and your nation today. Offer the prayer to me.

November 26

Revelation 22:17

• • •

The Spirit and the bride say, "Come."
And let everyone who hears say, "Come."
And let everyone who is thirsty come.
Let anyone who wishes take the water of life as a gift.

• • •

My children who lived in fear in the early church because of the evils of the Roman Empire got to this part of the book of Revelation and received this promise as a blessing. It said that one day they would know abundance and comfort because of their faith during scary times. Who are the people who are thirsty in your midst today? What water of life might you offer? What do you thirst for today? How might I offer the water of life in such a way that your thirst is quenched? Lift up that prayer to me today, that I might bless you as you bless others.

November 27

2 Chronicles 30:25-27

• • •

The whole assembly of Judah, the priests and the Levites, and the whole assembly that came out of Israel, and the resident aliens who came out of the land of Israel, and the resident aliens who lived in Judah, rejoiced. There was great joy in Jerusalem, for since the time of Solomon son of King David of Israel there had been nothing like this in Jerusalem. Then the priests and the Levites stood up and blessed the people, and their voice was heard; their prayer came to his holy dwelling in heaven.

• • •

If you want a glimpse of my Realm here on earth, this moment was such a glimpse. All the people came together in celebration: people of all faiths, people of diverse nations living together in the same city, people of all genders. And my designated priests blessed all the people and they prayed to me with joy and celebration and unity. This is the world I call on you to recreate, even if it be in glimpses.

November 28

Matthew 5:43–45

• • •

"You have heard that it was said, 'You shall love your neighbor and hate your enemy.' But I say to you, Love your enemies and pray for those who persecute you, so that you may be children of your Father in heaven; for he makes his sun rise on the evil and on the good, and sends rain on the righteous and on the unrighteous."

• • •

My Son invited his followers and invites you to one of the biggest leaps of faith imaginable: to extend compassion even to those who hate you. In this world, hate is sown so easily, and ignorance feeds it so effectively. The people who have been taught you are their enemy do not know you. Even the people who make your life difficult often do not know you. Build connection. Learn who they are and why they think they are against you. Really, most of my children want the same thing: to be known and loved and to feel safe. In other words, work to create a world where there are no enemies.

November 29

Ezra 9:15

• • •

"O Lord, God of Israel, you are just, but we have escaped as a remnant, as is now the case. Here we are before you in our guilt, though no one can face you because of this."

• • •

There have been times throughout history that are so brutal only some people survive. In those times the people who survive turn to me and say, "whatever we did that led to this, help us live a different way." Every time my guidance is the same: care for the least of these, live in humility and mutual care. Take care of each other. And your nation shall thrive and grow and know peace.

November 30

Mark 9:36–37

• • •

Then he took a little child and put it among them; and taking it in his arms, he said to them, "Whoever welcomes one such child in my name welcomes me, and whoever welcomes me welcomes not me but the one who sent me."

• • •

My littlest children are my greatest joy. In their best moments, they remember me better than any adult and reflect my love better. In their worst moments, they need their families' love to make them feel safe and to guide them into living in kindness and compassion. When your community invests itself in the thriving of children, including children not your own, you welcome me, and your community will likewise thrive.

December

Liberating Love
DEC

365 LOVE NOTES FROM GOD

December 1

Nehemiah 12:47

• • •

In the days of Zerubbabel and in the days of Nehemiah all Israel gave the daily portions for the singers and the gatekeepers. They set apart that which was for the Levites; and the Levites set apart that which was for the descendants of Aaron.

• • •

How does your community divide up its resources? What would reflect my priorities and my values? How much would go to the poor? How much would go to those providing spiritual care for you and creating worship experiences that connect you to the divine? How much would go to those in need? How much would stay in your community and how much would go to those outside? Use today's text to reflect on what a moral budget for your faith community would look like if it were to reflect my desires for you as a community.

December 2

Luke 9:57–58

• • •

As they were going along the road, someone said to him, "I will follow you wherever you go." And Jesus said to him, "Foxes have holes, and birds of the air have nests; but the Son of Man has nowhere to lay his head."

• • •

In one way, my Son was warning this man that following him meant sacrifice and discomfort; following him was not a whim, but something to be done with full commitment. In another way, though, he was reminding you to see how little you need when you follow him. Following Jesus means you already have everything you need. You have all the money, all the power, all the faith, and all the family you need already. Follow him and me now, bringing all that you have. Do not wait until you think you are ready or you will never follow. Know that you were born ready for this journey.

December 3

Esther 4:16

• • •

"Go, gather all the Jews to be found in Susa, and hold a fast on my behalf, and neither eat nor drink for three days, night or day. I and my maids will also fast as you do. After that I will go to the king, though it is against the law; and if I perish, I perish."

• • •

My beloved daughter Esther knew that she took a huge risk by telling her husband the king to protect the Jewish people from his advisor Haman's desire to massacre them. And so, knowing she might die for her action, she prepared herself spiritually, fasting for three days, to take this risk and do what was right. She also invited her supporters to join her in these spiritual preparations. When something hard is coming your way, what do you do to prepare yourself spiritually? Who do you invite to support you in doing the right thing?

December 4

John 13:34-35

• • •

"I give you a new commandment, that you love one another. Just as I have loved you, you also should love one another. By this everyone will know that you are my disciples, if you have love for one another."

• • •

Jesus showed his love in so many ways. He healed. He taught people how to worship and how to be community and how to share. He studied and debated scripture with great minds. He shed tears for those he loved. He disrupted acts of corruption and mistreatment of the poor. So today I ask you: when Jesus says to you "just as I have loved you, you also should love one another," how will you show love in the ways that Jesus did?

December 5

Job 38:28–29

• • •

"Has the rain a father,
    or who has begotten the drops of dew?
From whose womb did the ice come forth,
    and who has given birth to the hoarfrost of heaven?"

• • •

When Job came to me to boldly name his complaint about injustice in the world, I did not say he was wrong. He was right that this world is cruel to many people. What I reminded him was that he thought he had wealth and comfort because he worshiped me. In his privilege he had turned me into a magic genie, when in fact I am father to the oceans and mother to the mountains. I birthed this whole world and am much more vast and powerful than the wish-granter he thought he worshiped. Job has a lesson for all of my children: do not attribute someone's wealth to me, or anyone's suffering to me either. Remember instead that I journey with anyone who seeks to do my will in the world, and I will carry you into the next one.

December 6

Acts 12:6-7

• • •

The very night before Herod was going to bring him out, Peter, bound with two chains, was sleeping between two soldiers, while guards in front of the door were keeping watch over the prison. Suddenly an angel of the Lord appeared and a light shone in the cell. He tapped Peter on the side and woke him, saying, "Get up quickly." And the chains fell off his wrists.

• • •

I hope that when you read this story you are inspired by the miracles that carried the early church through such dangerous times. I hope you also ponder the ways angels show up in the whole Bible. In the gospels they show up as otherworldly, announcing my Son's birth. One showed up to Peter as a liberator in the most literal sense. In Genesis they show up looking like dusty, dirty travelers. If you are afraid of my radiance, you may miss your liberation. If you overlook my angels who are road-weary and rumpled, you may miss out again. Where are you letting in the divine to liberate you, however the angels appear?

December 7

Psalms 131:1–2

• • •

O LORD, my heart is not lifted up,
    my eyes are not raised too high;
I do not occupy myself with things
    too great and too marvelous for me.
But I have calmed and quieted my soul,
    like a weaned child with its mother;
    my soul within me is like a weaned child.

• • •

Sometimes the horrors of this world can overwhelm the most faithful of my children. It is absolutely okay to take time to turn inward, to quiet your soul, to focus on the small and beautiful things in your midst. Breathe, child. Find comfort in me, like a weaned child with its mother. The world needs you, but it needs you breathing and at peace in order to take on the changes that are yours to make. Today I invite you to take time to breathe, be still, and know that amidst the chaos, I am God and you are mine.

December 8

Romans 12:1–2

• • •

I appeal to you therefore, brothers and sisters, by the mercies of God, to present your bodies as a living sacrifice, holy and acceptable to God, which is your spiritual worship. Do not be conformed to this world, but be transformed by the renewing of your minds, so that you may discern what is the will of God—what is good and acceptable and perfect.

• • •

This world has staked a claim on your body. It has told you there is one kind of acceptable body, and that you need to change in order to be acceptable. When you offer your body to me, it is an act of liberation from the world's ways, because I know you to be beautiful and perfect as you are. This world seeks to crush the divine spark within you by telling you that you are not enough. Offer yourself to me, so that daily you can know that I love who you are in the world.

December 9

Proverbs 30:12-14

• • •

There are those who are pure in their own eyes
　　yet are not cleansed of their filthiness.
There are those—how lofty are their eyes,
　　how high their eyelids lift!—
there are those whose teeth are swords,
　　whose teeth are knives,
to devour the poor from off the earth,
　　the needy from among mortals.

• • •

Not everyone who claims to be aligned with my will necessarily is. This passage points out how to tell the difference. Is that person showing compassion for the poor and needy? If not, then no matter what they say or even believe, they have fallen away from me. You know who my true followers are; surround yourself with them so you are bolstered and strengthened by them. They will not be perfect any more than you are perfect, but they will help you build my kindom here on earth.

December 10

1 Corinthians 12:4-7

• • •

Now there are varieties of gifts, but the same Spirit; and there are varieties of services, but the same Lord; and there are varieties of activities, but it is the same God who activates all of them in everyone. To each is given the manifestation of the Spirit for the common good.

• • •

As you prepare for the arrival of my Son this season, it is a good time to reflect on gifts. Today I invite you to consider what spiritual gifts the various people around you have been given, and give thanks to me that they have been blessed in ways that are different from your own gifts. And consider the gifts I have given you—because you are glorious and those gifts shine inside of you—and give me thanks for blessing you in such a way that you are vital to the common good of your community.

December 11

Ecclesiastes 12:13–14

• • •

The end of the matter; all has been heard. Fear God, and keep his commandments; for that is the whole duty of everyone. For God will bring every deed into judgment, including every secret thing, whether good or evil.

• • •

Honoring me and following my commandments are all you are supposed to do. Leave the judging to me, because I have a better view of the whole picture. It seems that many people like to play God by judging and condemning. Those same people aren't very good at being human—of honoring me and following my path of love and compassion and care. May you find others who can be human with you for this journey I have called you to.

December 12

2 Corinthians 9:8–10

• • •

And God is able to provide you with every blessing in abundance, so that by always having enough of everything, you may share abundantly in every good work. As it is written,
    "He scatters abroad, he gives to the poor;
       his righteousness endures forever."
He who supplies seed to the sower and bread for food will supply and multiply your seed for sowing and increase the harvest of your righteousness.

• • •

As you await my Son's arrival, listen to these words from the church that emerged after his resurrection, which connected the church to its origins in the Hebrew Bible by quoting the Psalms. As I was in the beginning, as I was through my Son and through the early church, so am I today—a God who wants the flourishing of the least of these, which is why I sent my Son to you, and why I ask you to continue his work.

December 13

Song of Solomon 8:6-7

• • •

Set me as a seal upon your heart,
    as a seal upon your arm;
for love is strong as death,
    passion fierce as the grave.
Its flashes are flashes of fire,
    a raging flame.
Many waters cannot quench love,
    neither can floods drown it.
If one offered for love
    all the wealth of one's house,
    it would be utterly scorned.

• • •

May you know and be able to treasure the passion and love I created you for. May you know that those feelings are holy. May you know that you who embody this passion are holy.

December 14

Galatians 5:13–15

• • •

For you were called to freedom, brothers and sisters; only do not use your freedom as an opportunity for self-indulgence, but through love become slaves to one another. For the whole law is summed up in a single commandment, "You shall love your neighbor as yourself." If, however, you bite and devour one another, take care that you are not consumed by one another.

• • •

The word "slave" meant something very different in biblical times than the slavery created in the 1600s or the slavery happening today, with different codes and rules and causes. And it did mean to be of total service to the one who was your master. Which is the vibrant part of my son Paul's teaching here: if everyone is of total service to each other, no one can be master. Paul warned the church in Galatia that they were too busy picking at each other and undermining each other, trying to place themselves higher in a hierarchy that does not exist when I am at the center. Likewise, I want you to enjoy the freedom of serving each other, liberated from pettiness and competitiveness, but joined in community with my love as the foundation.

December 15

Isaiah 61:1-2

. . .

The spirit of the Lord GOD is upon me,
  because the LORD has anointed me;
he has sent me to bring good news to the oppressed,
  to bind up the brokenhearted,
to proclaim liberty to the captives,
  and release to the prisoners;
to proclaim the year of the LORD's favor,
  and the day of vengeance of our God;
  to comfort all who mourn.

. . .

You may know this passage as the one my Son read at the beginning of his ministry. He then stated that the blessing I bestowed upon my prophet so long before I had also bestowed on Him. My beautiful, powerful, kind, beloved child, I bestow this blessing also on you for the sake of my beloved community. Today I invite you to read this passage out loud as if you were the one who wrote it, and imagine how you will make this passage true of you.

December 16

Ephesians 4:31–32

• • •

Put away from you all bitterness and wrath and anger and wrangling and slander, together with all malice, and be kind to one another, tenderhearted, forgiving one another, as God in Christ has forgiven you.

• • •

This time of year is a double-edged sword for my Christ-following children. It is a time for messages of peace and generosity and family. It is also a time of frenzy and too many crowds and not enough time and too much pressure. Today I ask you to engage this passage from the letter to my early church in Ephesus as a prayer you lift up to me: "God, help me put away all bitterness. Help me put away all wrath. Help me put away all anger...(through the list), and help me be kind to others, help me be tenderhearted, help me forgive others as you have forgiven me." After each sentence, breathe in my Spirit and breathe out the stress the world generates for you.

December 17

Jeremiah 31:3-4b

• • •

...the LORD appeared to him from far away.
I have loved you with an everlasting love;
    therefore I have continued my faithfulness to you...
Again you shall take your tambourines,
    and go forth in the dance of the merrymakers.

• • •

Your ancestors treated the days leading up to Christmas as a time of fasting, penitence, and preparation as they anticipated my child born among them. Those practices honor me and ground my children. I wish this season were still treated as a holy and meditative time of preparation, but I also want you always to find joy in me. There can be joy in anticipation and preparation. There can be joy in meditation. For the sake of a world that needs joy, I invite you, like your ancestors whom Jeremiah promised would see a better day because of my love, to go forth in the dance of merrymakers. May your joy today at my love be so great that it is visible to those around you.

December 18

Philippians 4:4-7

. . .

Rejoice in the Lord always; again I will say, Rejoice. Let your gentleness be known to everyone. The Lord is near. Do not worry about anything, but in everything by prayer and supplication with thanksgiving let your requests be made known to God. And the peace of God, which surpasses all understanding, will guard your hearts and your minds in Christ Jesus.

. . .

My beloved child who wrote this letter wanted his church to be a beacon and inspiration to those in need of hope. Today I invite you to read this letter as it was written: to a group. Imagine it has been written to your faith community. If it helps, add the phrase "you all," to remember the writer was inviting a whole community to rejoice together, not placing that burden on one person who might not be able to do so. He was inviting the whole community to be known for its gentleness, so that on a day when any singular person might not be the embodiment of gentleness, the rest of the community could step up. I made you for community so that you do not have to be Christ to the world all by yourself, but that your community can support each other in being Christ to the world.

December 19

Lamentations 5:19–21

• • •

But you, O Lord, reign forever;
    your throne endures to all generations.
Why have you forgotten us completely?
    Why have you forsaken us these many days?
Restore us to yourself, O Lord, that we may be restored;
    renew our days as of old.

• • •

In hard times my beloved children may feel as if I am not present. It was true in the time of Lamentations, and it was true in the time before my Son came. Some people worry about disrespecting me by challenging me in this way. But only those who see me as true family—as your beloved parent—have the courage to call out to me to show up in ways you can see. Today I invite you to be brave and share with me what in your community is breaking your heart, and demand that I provide healing. My spirit might whisper a word of support or guidance to you if you listen. Also, I am not fragile. I can hold your pain for and with you just as I did for my children Israel.

December 20

Colossians 3:14–15

• • •

Above all, clothe yourselves with love, which binds everything together in perfect harmony. And let the peace of Christ rule in your hearts, to which indeed you were called in the one body. And be thankful.

• • •

Today I want to offer you a playful request: what does it look like when you are clothed with love? Are you decked out in vibrant neon or cool forest colors? Is it sparkles or silk or denim? Do the clothes look different depending on the occasion? How will you clothe yourself with love today so that everyone admires your wardrobe? (And when they do, let them know you got your clothes from me...they are priceless.)

December 21

Ezekiel 44:28–30

• • •

This shall be their inheritance: I am their inheritance; and you shall give them no holding in Israel; I am their holding. They shall eat the grain offering, the sin offering, and the guilt offering; and every devoted thing in Israel shall be theirs. The first of all the first fruits of all kinds, and every offering of all kinds from all your offerings, shall belong to the priests; you shall also give to the priests the first of your dough, in order that a blessing may rest on your house.

• • •

The Levites (priests) who remained faithful to me when so many others were seduced by idols and corruption were given honor by me in this time. And yet the way they were honored did not involve inheriting wealth or building up capital. Even in those days I tried to show that the closer one is to God, the less connection one has to the accumulation of wealth. Who are the people in your life who are close to me and do not focus on gaining land or inheritance, who see me as their inheritance? What are you offering them as support so that a blessing may rest on your house?

December 22

1 Thessalonians 5:15–22

• • •

See that none of you repays evil for evil, but always seek to do good to one another and to all. Rejoice always, pray without ceasing, give thanks in all circumstances; for this is the will of God in Christ Jesus for you. Do not quench the Spirit. Do not despise the words of prophets, but test everything; hold fast to what is good; abstain from every form of evil.

• • •

One of my beloved children once said, "bringing your whole heart to the church should not mean checking your brain at the door." My child who wrote this letter wanted the church to remain open to the constant moving of my Spirit in all of her constantly alive and current ways. He also wanted the church to turn to the ancient wisdom of the prophets who came before, who were also trying to guide communities to follow me. And finally, he wanted the church to take all of its experiences and its texts and measure them against my greatest teachings of love, compassion, and care, filtering out that which does not serve those teachings. Today I invite you to bring this same philosophy to your community of faith, so that you can hold fast to what is good and more easily abstain from every form of evil.

December 23

Daniel 12:10,13

• • •

"Many shall be purified, cleansed, and refined, but the wicked shall continue to act wickedly. None of the wicked shall understand, but those who are wise shall understand...But you, go your way, and rest; you shall rise for your reward at the end of the days."

• • •

As you grow closer to the day of my Son's birth, remember that some of my children claim today as "Little Christmas Eve," in which they exchange books and stay in to read all day. For all of your hard work, you also deserve to rest. In your service of me, you will save some people from great harm to themselves. Some people committed to evil will remain committed. You will be misunderstood by some and deeply valued by others. And at the end of all of that, I will embrace you with such love and welcome. So for now, find a moment to breathe and recharge.

December 24

2 Thessalonians 3:14–16

• • •

Take note of those who do not obey what we say in this letter; have nothing to do with them, so that they may be ashamed. Do not regard them as enemies, but warn them as believers. Now may the Lord of peace himself give you peace at all times in all ways. The Lord be with all of you.

• • •

Even when you know someone is in the wrong, you can choose not to make them an enemy. The stakes were very high for the church in Thessalonika. Even so, they were encouraged to give people a chance to do right instead of condemning them as evil. On the eve of the birth of my Son, the Prince of Peace, who did not even condemn those who mocked and sought to kill him, reflect on who in your life could be engaged as a sibling in need rather than as an enemy. Pray to me for help in changing your heart about them.

December 25

Hosea 14:2b-3

• • •

"Take away all guilt;
    accept that which is good,
    and we will offer
    the fruit of our lips.
Assyria shall not save us;
    we will not ride upon horses;
we will say no more, 'Our God,'
    to the work of our hands.
In you the orphan finds mercy."

• • •

On this birthday of my Son, I invite you to turn to an ancient text from which He would have studied and learned. As you celebrate Him today, reflect on what it means to give up believing that the work of your hands or a strong army is your salvation. Instead, embrace me, the God of the orphan and of the innocent and sinner, the God of a baby born vulnerable among animals brought in from the cold and born of his teenage mother and his father who also wasn't his father, the God of the family who took in a very pregnant woman and of the many people who would not. I ask you today to offer me "the fruit of [your] lips," the songs of your heart.

December 26

1 Timothy 6:17–19

• • •

As for those who in the present age are rich, command them not to be haughty, or to set their hopes on the uncertainty of riches, but rather on God who richly provides us with everything for our enjoyment. They are to do good, to be rich in good works, generous, and ready to share, thus storing up for themselves the treasure of a good foundation for the future, so that they may take hold of the life that really is life.

• • •

I am well-known as the God of the poor, but that does not mean I have given up on my children of wealth. There are paths to redemption for everyone, including them. My beloved Son sat often with people of wealth, but if they rejected the poor, he had no patience for them. Worldly goods are temporary and fickle. I am the better long-term bet. And to bet on me means not only giving money but also engaging in service to those in need. Those who follow this path, whether rich or poor, set themselves on a path to an eternity with me, starting right now.

December 27

Joel 3:16

• • •

The LORD roars from Zion,
>and utters his voice from Jerusalem,
>and the heavens and the earth shake.
But the LORD is a refuge for his people,
>a stronghold for the people of Israel.

• • •

People are afraid of me, of what I can do. They are so afraid that they blame me for things I did not do. But as the prophet Joel reminded his people, no matter how afraid they are of my wrath, I am also a refuge for my people. Whatever you need refuge from, turn to me. I love you and want your thriving. When you have failed, I will be there to pick you up. When you feel vulnerable, I will be there to comfort you. When you celebrate, I will celebrate with you. When you heal my children, you are doing the same to me. I will always be with you.

December 28

2 Timothy 3:2-5

• • •

For people will be lovers of themselves, lovers of money, boasters, arrogant, abusive, disobedient to their parents, ungrateful, unholy, inhuman, implacable, slanderers, profligates, brutes, haters of good, treacherous, reckless, swollen with conceit, lovers of pleasure rather than lovers of God, holding to the outward form of godliness but denying its power. Avoid them!

• • •

Today I will let my child's writing speak for itself and simply invite you to pray for protection from each of these behaviors in yourself and in your community, and pray for protection from those who exhibit these behaviors.

December 29

Amos 9:13b–15

• • •

...the mountains shall drip sweet wine,
and all the hills shall flow with it.
I will restore the fortunes of my people Israel,
and they shall rebuild the ruined cities and inhabit
them;
they shall plant vineyards and drink their wine,
and they shall make gardens and eat their fruit.
I will plant them upon their land,
and they shall never again be plucked up
out of the land that I have given them,
says the LORD your God.

• • •

This is the promise my beloved child and prophet Amos gave to the people of Israel after warning them of the costs of rejecting my will and seeking an easy and sinful path instead. In a world where my children follow my will, you will thrive and live glorious lives and will know comfort and ease and stability. Today I make this promise to you: if your community lives faithfully in my ways of love, care, and compassion, you will all know this level of ease.

December 30

Titus 3:8–9

• • •

I desire that you insist on these things, so that those who have come to believe in God may be careful to devote themselves to good works; these things are excellent and profitable to everyone. But avoid stupid controversies, genealogies, dissensions, and quarrels about the law, for they are unprofitable and worthless.

• • •

As one of my beloved children said, "Major in the majors and minor in the minors." Focus on the most important things, and be clear on what they are, so people know what kind of community you are building. Make sure people know what it means to live in service to each other, to care for those in need, to recognize the divine in each other and also in yourself so that you really can love others as you love yourself because you really do love yourself. When your community is clear on what it is about, it can let go of the small quibbles that take up so much space when a community is confused about its purpose. My beloved child, I am counting on you to help your community major in the majors.

December 31

Psalm 107:8–9

• • •

Let them thank the LORD for his steadfast love,
    for his wonderful works to humankind.
For he satisfies the thirsty,
    and the hungry he fills with good things.

• • •

Today I invite you to turn in your Bible to Psalm 107 and read the whole Psalm. As you prepare for a new year with untold adventures and joys and losses and heartbreak, take heart in the fact that you remain faithful to a God who "pours contempt on princes...[and] raises up the needy out of distress." I liberate people from prison and rescue people from natural disasters and care for those who are sick and vindicate those who have been mistreated...and I do it through you. I am in you. You are my vessel. I treasure you so much. Know always that you are my beloved child, in whom I am well pleased.

Conclusion

I didn't even realize that the prayer I had on a loop in the back of my head while I was writing this was a prayer by one of the world's favorite monks, Thomas Merton in his *Thoughts in Solitude*:

> My Lord God, I have no idea where I am going. I do not see the road ahead of me. I cannot know for certain where it will end. Nor do I really know myself, and the fact that I think I am following your will does not mean that I am actually doing so. But I believe that the desire to please you does in fact please you. And I hope I have that desire in all that I am doing. I hope that I will never do anything apart from that desire. And I know that if I do this you will lead me by the right road, though I may know nothing about it. Therefore I will trust you always though I may seem to be lost and in the shadow of death. I will not fear, for you are ever with me, and you will never leave me to face my perils alone.

I felt both humble(d) and embarrassed by my cockiness in attempting this, especially writing it as if it was written by God. But I wanted people to feel the intimacy that I think is at the heart of Christian faith. And so this prayer unconsciously swirled around me with every devotion I wrote.

I knew that not everything would resonate with everyone—since I worked my way through every book of the Bible, I sometimes ended up choosing passages that really challenged me and that I would rather have ignored. I think for everyone who engages the texts with humility and openness, that happens. (If you were looking for the pattern, it went like this: Day 1, Hebrew Bible Book One; Day 2, New Testament Book One; Day 3, Hebrew Bible Book Two; Day 4, New Testament Book Two and so on. This gave me somewhere between five and eight passages from every single book of the Bible. There were a couple of glitches where I miscounted or where a whole book of the Bible had so few verses I ran out of material and had to steal from a Psalm.) And since I believe each text can be interpreted numerous ways for what is needed in a current context, I hope that if my interpretation wasn't meaningful, you were able to let God shine through the scripture for that day in a different way.

In addition to Thomas Merton's prayer, the other voice in my head (besides, I hope, the voice of God) was that of my friends who are Bible scholars. I knew that they would be disgusted by some of my gross misinterpretations of the text, but I also knew that they would have compassion for the purpose of a devotional, which is not the same purpose as rigorous contextual analysis of the scripture. I tried to do right by them insofar as I could, because their work has helped the complicated figures of the Bible come alive and become relevant to me in a way that literal readings of the text never really helped me do. I hope they forgive me my many errors and I hope you will plunge into every womanist biblical interpretation book you can find so you can re-meet our spiritual ancestors in ways that will feed you more than this book ever could.

This book was a God-given gift to me in so many ways, as a lover of Jesus and as a nerd in equal measures: As I studied the texts, learned about Sanballat the Horonite and the timeline of Jerusalem's conquests, I rediscovered the joy of reading and deeply studying the text and letting its messages of compassion and liberation reveal themselves (sometimes hidden because of metaphors no longer used, sometimes hidden because even the authors of these texts, like me, cannot fully comprehend how amazing God is). And then as I reposted on social media the devotions I had written months before, the devotions spoke words of comfort and encouragement to me even though I had been the one to write them.

A sermon I heard by Rev. Dr. Donna Allen about Hagar in 2016 gave me courage with a few risky passages where I may have stretched standard interpretations a little bit. The book of Genesis said that Hagar tried to escape enslavement once, but God told her to return and she was obedient, and then much later Abraham cast her and their son out at the demand of his wife Sarah, jealous of how smug the fertile Hagar had become. Dr. Allen (possibly the best preacher in the Bay Area and one of the best biblical interpreters I know) preached that the God she worships does not send people back to enslavement, so she did what my Jewish scholar friends might call midrash—the storytelling of what happens in between what is written in the Bible. Dr. Allen said she imagined that it was against the interest of the author to admit this, but Hagar attempted to escape, and when she was caught and brought back, she thought, "OK. That was a little reconnaissance for the next time I get out of here." And that wisdom helped her survive when she was thrown out by the father of her child.

I remember hearing that sermon (available on the First Congregational Church of Oakland website, and worth every minute of the almost one-hour sermon) and being shocked that she was simply disagreeing with what was written in the text rather than reinterpreting it. And then I thought, "but I also know that my God would never send someone back to enslavement." So if I took a couple of liberties in my interpretation of texts that condone behavior I know God rejects, I thank Dr. Allen for the courage to do so. I believe I was trying to honor God in the process, and I believe that my trying to please God pleases God.

Lastly, my hope is that this devotional helped you reread familiar passages in new ways, particularly in relationship to how the Bible is most of all a book on how to be community together as God intended. I believe one of the greatest sins of the modern era is the sin of propagating individualism, which is so nefarious that it even creeps into how we read the scripture. I hope that you feel reinvigorated to be about the work of building God's Beloved Community here on earth by the end of this year's journey. Thank you for going on it with me, and with God.

Index

Genesis
Genesis 1:1–3, 1
Genesis 18:1–3, 75
Genesis 21:17–19, 153
Genesis 33:4, 230
Genesis 39:23, 306

Exodus
Exodus 1:15–17, 3
Exodus 3:11–12, 77
Exodus 13:17–18a, 155
Exodus 22:25–27, 232
Exodus 40:36–38, 308

Leviticus
Leviticus 19:18, 234
Leviticus 19:32, 5
Leviticus 19:33–34, 79
Leviticus 19:35–36, 157
Leviticus 22:20, 310

Numbers
Numbers 5:5–7, 7
Numbers 8:23–25, 81
Numbers 10:29, 159
Numbers 11:10–12, 236
Numbers 30:1–2, 312

Deuteronomy
Deuteronomy 1:17a, 9
Deuteronomy 1:31, 83
Deuteronomy 4:9, 161
Deuteronomy 4:31, 238
Deuteronomy 4:39, 314

Joshua
Joshua 1:5, 11
Joshua 6:18, 85
Joshua 20:1–3, 163
Joshua 22:26–27, 240
Joshua 24:15, 316

Judges
Judges 5:23 (Song of Deborah), 13
Judges 6:7–10, 87
Judges 10:11–14, 165

Judges 11:1–2, 242
Judges 11:39–40, 318

Ruth
Ruth 1:16–17, 15
Ruth 1:20b–21, 89
Ruth 2:8–9, 167
Ruth 2:20, 244
Ruth 4:14–15, 320

1 Samuel
1 Samuel 1:12–16, 17
1 Samuel 3:8–9, 91
1 Samuel 3:12–13, 169
1 Samuel 8:6–8, 245
1 Samuel 12:19–21, 322

2 Samuel
2 Samuel 5:1–2, 19
2 Samuel 5:12, 92
2 Samuel 6:20b–22, 171
2 Samuel 7:18–19, 247
2 Samuel 12:5–7;9a, 324

1 Kings
1 Kings 2:1–3, 21
1 Kings 3:7–9, 94
1 Kings 3:25–27, 173
1 Kings 8:41–43, 249
1 Kings 19:11b–13, 326

2 Kings
2 Kings 1:2–3, 23
2 Kings 2:11–12, 96
2 Kings 4:42–44, 175
2 Kings 5:11–14, 251
2 Kings 12:13–14, 328

1 Chronicles
1 Chronicles 1:1–7, 25
1 Chronicles 15:16, 98
1 Chronicles 21:17, 177
1 Chronicles 22:2–5, 253
1 Chronicles 29:14–18, 330

2 Chronicles
2 Chronicles 5:13–14, 27

2 Chronicles 13:18, 100
2 Chronicles 24:20, 179
2 Chronicles 30:8–9, 255
2 Chronicles 30:25–27, 332

Ezra
Ezra 1:2–4, 29
Ezra 3:11b–13, 102
Ezra 6:20b–22, 181
Ezra 7:27–28, 257
Ezra 9:15, 334

Nehemiah
Nehemiah 1:8–11, 31
Nehemiah 2:17–20a, 183
Nehemiah 2:17b–20a, 104
Nehemiah 8:9–10, 259
Nehemiah 12:47, 336

Esther
Esther 1:17b–18, 32
Esther 2:19–20, 106
Esther 3:2–3, 185
Esther 4:13b–14 , 261
Esther 4:16, 338

Job
Job 1:20–21, 34
Job 10:2–3, 108
Job 16:2–4 , 187
Job 24:2–4, 263
Job 38:28–29, 340

Psalm
Psalm 107:8–9, 366
Psalms 17:7–10, 36
Psalms 25:14–15, 110
Psalms 33:20–21, 152
Psalms 71:17–19, 189
Psalms 102:25–28, 265
Psalms 131:1–2, 342

Proverbs
Proverbs 1:20–22, 38
Proverbs 8:1–6, 112
Proverbs 20:3, 191
Proverbs 28:1, 267
Proverbs 30:12–14, 344

Ecclesiastes
Ecclesiastes 1:9–10, 40
Ecclesiastes 3:1–4, 114
Ecclesiastes 4:1, 4, 193
Ecclesiastes 9:13–18, 269
Ecclesiastes 12:13–14, 346

Song of Solomon
Song of Solomon 1:5, 116
Song of Solomon 1:15–16a, 195
Song of Solomon 2:10–12, 271
Song of Solomon 8:6–7, 348

Isaiah
Isaiah 40:1–2, 42
Isaiah 42:13–14, 118
Isaiah 43:8–9, 197
Isaiah 54:13–14, 273
Isaiah 61:1–2, 350

Jeremiah
Jeremiah 6:13–14, 44
Jeremiah 17:5–6a, 7–8a, 120
Jeremiah 29:11–14a, 199
Jeremiah 30:17, 275
Jeremiah 31:3–4b, 352

Lamentations
Lamentations 1:1, 46
Lamentations 1:18, 122
Lamentations 2:13, 201
Lamentations 3:25–28,31–33, 277
Lamentations 5:19–21, 354

Ezekiel
Ezekiel 16:49, 48
Ezekiel 18:1–3, 124
Ezekiel 18:21–23, 203
Ezekiel 37:1–3a, 279
Ezekiel 44:28–30, 356

Daniel
Daniel 3:16–18, 50
Daniel 6:26b–27, 126
Daniel 9:16–17, 205
Daniel 9:18–19, 281
Daniel 12:10,13, 358

Hosea
Hosea 5:14b–15, 52
Hosea 6:3, 128
Hosea 7:8–10, 207
Hosea 10:13–14a , 283
Hosea 14:2b–3, 360

Joel

Joel 2:1–2, 130
Joel 2:12–13, 54
Joel 2:28–29, 209
Joel 3:14, 285
Joel 3:16, 362

Amos

Amos 2:11–12, 56
Amos 5:11–12, 132
Amos 5:15, 211
Amos 5:23–24, 287
Amos 9:13b–15, 364

Obadiah

Obadiah 1:3–4, 58
Obadiah 1:6–7, 134
Obadiah 1:15, 289
Obadiah:11–12, 213

Jonah

Jonah 1:1–3, 60
Jonah 2:1–2, 136
Jonah 4:2, 214
Jonah 4:10b–11, 291

Micah

Micah 3:5, 61
Micah 4:3–4, 138
Micah 5:7, 216
Micah 6:7–8, 293

Nahum

Nahum 1:7–8a, 63
Nahum 1:15, 140
Nahum 3:8, 10a , 218
Nahum 3:19, 295

Habakkuk

Habakkuk 1:2–4, 65
Habakkuk 1:13, 142
Habakkuk 2:2–3, 220
Habakkuk 2:4–5, 297

Zephaniah

Zephaniah 1:7–9, 67
Zephaniah 1:12–13, 144
Zephaniah 2:3, 222
Zephaniah 3:1–2, 299

Haggai

Haggai 1:7–8, 69
Haggai 2:4–5, 146
Haggai 2:6–7, 224
Haggai 2:18b–19, 301

Zechariah

Zechariah 1:3–4, 71
Zechariah 9:9, 148
Zechariah 10:6, 226
Zechariah 12:10, 303

Malachi

Malachi 1:10a, 73
Malachi 1:11, 150
Malachi 3:6–7a, 228
Malachi 4:5–6, 305

Matthew

Matthew 2:13–15, 2
Matthew 3:1–3, 57
Matthew 3:16–17, 113
Matthew 4:1–4, 168
Matthew 5:5, 223
Matthew 5:23–24, 278
Matthew 5:43–45, 333

Mark

Mark 1:16–18, 4
Mark 3:31–35, 59
Mark 4:21–22, 115
Mark 5:33–34, 170
Mark 8:34–35, 225
Mark 9:35, 280
Mark 9:36–37, 335

Luke

Luke 2:48–49, 6
Luke 5:30–32, 62
Luke 6:20b–21, 117
Luke 6:36, 172
Luke 6:49, 227
Luke 7:33–35, 282
Luke 9:57–58, 337

John

John 1:5, 8
John 2:15–16, 107
John 3:8, 64
John 4:27, 119
John 6:15, 174
John 7:52, 229

John 12:35–36, 284
John 13:34–35, 339
John 20:18, 272
John 20:27–29, 274
John 21:15, 327
John 21:20–22, 329

Acts

Acts 2:44–45, 10
Acts 4:13, 66
Acts 5:38–39, 121
Acts 7:51–53, 176
Acts 8:36–38, 231
Acts 10:25–28, 286
Acts 12:6–7, 341

Romans

Romans 2:2–4, 12
Romans 3:27–28, 68
Romans 5:3–5, 123
Romans 6:4, 178
Romans 7:15, 233
Romans 8:22–25, 288
Romans 12:1–2, 343

1 Corinthians

1 Corinthians 2:1–3, 14
1 Corinthians 4:1–2, 70
1 Corinthians 5:6–7a, 125
1 Corinthians 6:12, 180
1 Corinthians 9:25, 235
1 Corinthians 11:20–22a, 290
1 Corinthians 12:4–7, 345

2 Corinthians

2 Corinthians 2:15, 16
2 Corinthians 4:7–10, 72
2 Corinthians 5:1, 127
2 Corinthians 6:11–13, 182
2 Corinthians 8:9–11, 237
2 Corinthians 9:6–7, 292
2 Corinthians 9:8–10, 347

Galatians

Galatians 1:3–5, 18
Galatians 1:10, 74
Galatians 2:9–10, 129
Galatians 3:1–2, 184
Galatians 4:13–14, 239

Galatians 5:1, 294
Galatians 5:13–15, 349

Ephesians

Ephesians 2:4–7, 20
Ephesians 2:17–19, 76
Ephesians 3:13, 131
Ephesians 3:20–21, 186
Ephesians 4:11–12, 241
Ephesians 4:25–27, 296
Ephesians 4:31–32, 351

Philippians

Philippians 1:27–28a, 22
Philippians 2:1–2, 78
Philippians 2:3–4, 133
Philippians 2:5–8, 188
Philippians 2:14–15, 243
Philippians 3:18–20, 298
Philippians 4:4–7, 353

Colossians

Colossians 1:11–12, 24
Colossians 2:2–3, 80
Colossians 2:6–7, 135
Colossians 3:1–2, 246
Colossians 3:8–11, 300
Colossians 3:14–15, 355
Colossians 4:5–6, 190

1 Thessalonians

1 Thessalonians 4:1, 26
1 Thessalonians 4:9, 82
1 Thessalonians 4:10–12, 137
1 Thessalonians 5:1–2, 192
1 Thessalonians 5:9–11, 248
1 Thessalonians 5:12–13, 302
1 Thessalonians 5:15–22, 357

2 Thessalonians

2 Thessalonians 1:3, 28
2 Thessalonians 1:11–12, 84
2 Thessalonians 2:1–2, 139
2 Thessalonians 2:9–10, 194
2 Thessalonians 2:16–17, 250
2 Thessalonians 3:13, 304
2 Thessalonians 3:14–16, 359

1 Timothy

1 Timothy 1:15, 30

1 Timothy 3:16b, 86
1 Timothy 4:4–5, 141
1 Timothy 4:12, 196
1 Timothy 5:1–2, 252
1 Timothy 6:11–12, 307
1 Timothy 6:17–19, 361

2 Timothy
2 Timothy 1:6–7, 33
2 Timothy 1:8–9a, 88
2 Timothy 2:8–9, 143
2 Timothy 2:11–13, 198
2 Timothy 2:14b–15, 254
2 Timothy 2:16, 309
2 Timothy 3:2–5, 363

Titus
Titus 1:7, 35
Titus 1:8, 90
Titus 1:15–16a, 145
Titus 2:11–13, 200
Titus 3:3–5, 256
Titus 3:6–7, 311
Titus 3:8–9, 365

Philemon
Philemon 1:3–5, 37
Philemon 1:6, 93
Philemon 1:7, 147
Philemon 1:8–9a, 202
Philemon 1:15–16, 258
Philemon 1:17–18, 313

Hebrews
Hebrews 2:16, 39
Hebrews 4:15, 95
Hebrews 5:13–14, 149
Hebrews 6:10, 260
Hebrews 13:1–3, 315

James
James 1:2–4, 41
James 1:19–21, 97
James 1:22–25, 151
James 1:26–27, 206
James 2:1–4, 204
James 2:5–7, 262
James 2:14–18, 317
James 5:4–5, 270

James 5:7–8, 325

1 Peter
1 Peter 2:1–3, 43
1 Peter 2:4–6, 99
1 Peter 2:9–10, 154
1 Peter 2:23–25, 208
1 Peter 4:8–11, 264
1 Peter 5:6–9, 319

2 Peter
2 Peter 1:3, 45
2 Peter 1:5–8, 101
2 Peter 1:10–11, 156
2 Peter 2:18–19, 210
2 Peter 3:8–9, 266
2 Peter 3:13–15a, 321

1 John
1 John 1:8–10, 47
1 John 2:4–6, 103
1 John 3:18–20, 158
1 John 4:18–21, 212
1 John 5:2–5, 268
1 John 5:20, 323

2 John
2 John 1:3, 49
2 John 1:5, 105
2 John 1:6, 160
2 John 1:8, 215

3 John
3 John 1:3–4, 51
3 John 1:5–6a, 162
3 John 1:11, 217

Jude
Jude 1:20, 53
Jude 1:21, 109
Jude 1:22–23, 164
Jude 1:24–25, 219

Revelation
Revelation 2:4–5a, 55
Revelation 3:1b–3, 111
Revelation 3:15–17, 166
Revelation 22:1–2, 221
Revelation 22:5, 276
Revelation 22:17, 331